BEAT!
LCA English Assignments Workbook

NESSA McDONAGH

Gill & Macmillan

Gill & Macmillan
Hume Avenue
Park West
Dublin 12
with associated companies throughout the world
www.gillmacmillan.ie

© Nessa McDonagh 2011
Design by Liz White Designs, Wicklow
Print origination by TypeIt, Dublin

978 07171 4873 8

The paper used in this book is made from the wood pulp of managed forests. For every tree felled, at least one tree is planted, thereby renewing natural resources.

All rights reserved.
No part of this publication may be copied, reproduced or transmitted in any form or by any means without written permission of the publishers or else under the terms of any licence permitting limited copying issued by the Irish Copyright Licensing Agency.

Any links to external websites should not be construed as an endorsement by Gill & Macmillan of the content or view of the linked material.

For permission to reproduce photographs, the author and publisher gratefully acknowledge the following:

© Advertising Archives: 66, 70; © Alamy: 27, 143, 150, 159, 165, 185, 196, 201, 212; © Collins Agency: 132; © Corbis: 19, 29; © Getty: 1, 2, 6, 8, 12, 55, 77, 168, 173; © Photocall Ireland!: 120; © Photolibrary: 105, 154; © Rex Features: 21, 40, 153; © RTÉ: 68; Courtesy of Bauer Media: 144; Courtesy of Clare Champion: 106CL; Courtesy of Evening Herald: 106CR; Courtesy of Irish Times: 106L, 108; Courtesy of The Sunday Business Post: 106R.

The authors and publisher have made every effort to trace all copyright holders, but if any has been inadvertently overlooked we would be pleased to make the necessary arrangement at the first opportunity.

CONTENTS

Module 1 Communication and the Working World

Chapter 1	Introduction to Communication	2
Chapter 2	Listening Skills	8
Chapter 3	Telephone Techniques	12
Chapter 4	Writing a Report	19
Chapter 5	Writing a Review	26
Chapter 6	Curriculum Vitae and Letter Writing Skills	41
	End of Module Checklist	54

Module 2 Communication and Enterprise

Chapter 7	Introduction to Enterprise	56
Chapter 8	Advertising	64
Chapter 9	Setting up a Mini-company	73
	End of Module Checklist	104

Module 3 The Communications Media

Chapter 10	Newspapers	106
Chapter 11	Radio	120
Chapter 12	Television	132
Chapter 13	Aspects of Film	144
	End of Module Checklist	152

Module 4 Critical Literacy and Composition

Chapter 14	The Poetry of Popular Song	154
Chapter 15	Poetry	165
Chapter 16	Short Story	173
Chapter 17	Novel	185
Chapter 18	Drama and Theatre	196
Chapter 19	Film Studies	212
	End of Module Checklist	216

| Chapter 20 | Revision | 217 |

Module ONE

Communication and the Working World

CHAPTER 1 Introduction to Communication

1. Explain what is meant by the term 'communication'.

   _____
   _____
   _____
   _____
   _____

2. When referring to communication, what do the terms 'sender' and 'receiver' mean?

   _____
   _____
   _____
   _____

3. What is a 'barrier' to communication? Give examples with your answer.

   _____
   _____
   _____
   _____

4. Describe three different forms of written communication.

   (a) _____
   _____

   (b) _____
   _____

   (c) _____
   _____

5. Describe three forms of verbal communication.

   (a) _____

   (b) _____

   (c) _____

6. Describe three forms of non-verbal communication.

   (a) _____

   (b) _____

   (c) _____

7. What is meant by 'ineffective communication'?

   _____
   _____
   _____
   _____

8. Describe a situation that occurs in your school where you think communication is ineffective.

   _____
   _____
   _____
   _____

9. How would you make this communication more effective?

   _____
   _____
   _____
   _____

10. Read the extract below and answer the questions that follow.

> An old man went to the post office to buy a stamp for a letter. The cashier handed him the stamp. He took the stamp, licked the back of it and pressed it down on the envelope.
>
> 'This won't stick,' he told the cashier, as he pressed it firmly onto the letter.
>
> 'You have to peel the paper off the back of it,' the cashier instructed him.
>
> 'What?' he asked, still struggling with the stamp.
>
> 'Peel the paper off the back,' she instructed him again.
>
> The old man did as he was told. He carefully peeled the paper off the back, licked the stamp again and pressed it onto the envelope.
>
> 'It still won't stick,' he said impatiently.
>
> 'It's a self-stick stamp,' the cashier replied.
>
> 'Well this one isn't sticking at all – there's something wrong with it,' said the old man crossly.
>
> 'It won't stick now because you've licked it. Just give it here and I'll post it for you,' said the cashier, taking the stamp and the envelope. 'These new stamps don't need licking,' she continued, realising the old man was confused. 'They're self-sticking. They save time. They're already sticky.'
>
> The old man looked blankly.
>
> 'Look,' said the cashier, trying to explain, 'just imagine they've already been licked.'
>
> At that, the man's face fell and he scurried out the door in search of a chemist to buy some mouthwash!

(a) Why did the old man lick the stamp?

_____

_____

(b) Why was the stamp not sticking to the envelope?

_____

_____

(c) The cashier told the old man to peel the paper off the back of the stamp. What was wrong with her instruction?

_____

_____

_____

_____

(d) Why did the old man run off looking for mouthwash?

(e) What instructions would you give to the old man to help him stick the stamp on the envelope?

11.

CD - Track 1

(a) Listen to Track 1 on the CD. Describe the style of music that you hear.

(b) What instruments are being played in this piece?

(c) Describe the tempo (speed) of the piece.

(d) What mood do you think this piece of music communicates? Explain your answer.

12. Imagine that you have been asked to select a particular piece of music for a film of your choice.

(a) Describe the piece of music you have chosen. (i.e. tempo, style, genre etc.)

_____
_____
_____

(b) What is it that you particularly like about this piece of music?

_____
_____
_____

(c) What mood does this piece of music communicate?

_____
_____

(d) Describe what action would be taking place on screen while this music played in the background. Explain your answer.

_____
_____
_____
_____

13. What is meant by body language?

_____
_____
_____

14. In your own words, explain the facial expressions and body language associated with the emotions listed below.

> ### Example!
>
> **ANGRY**
> **Facial expressions:** Red face, frown, clenched teeth, pinched lips.
> **Body language:** Folded arms, a pointing finger, loud breathing, pacing the floor.

(a) **HAPPY**

Facial expressions: _____

_____

Body language: _____

_____

(b) **AFRAID**

Facial expressions: _____

_____

Body language: _____

_____

(c) **SHOCKED**

Facial expressions: _____

_____

Body language: _____

_____

(d) **EMBARRASSED**

Facial expressions: _____

_____

Body language: _____

_____

PRACTICAL EXERCISE!

Practise body language techniques by playing a game of charades. This is an acting game in which one player *acts out* a word or phrase and the other players guess the meaning. The idea is to use physical rather than verbal language to convey the meaning to another group. Have fun! ☺

CHAPTER 2 Listening Skills

1. Explain three reasons why listening is important.

    (a) _____
    _____
    _____

    (b) _____
    _____
    _____

    (c) _____
    _____

2. **CD - Track 2**

    The conversation below appears as Track 2 on the CD. Listen to the track, *without reading the conversation*, and try to answer the questions.

    Next, try reading the conversation first and then answering the questions. Which is easier? Why?

    John and Helen are talking outside the shopping centre.

    John: Kevin has just moved house. He lives on Collins Road now, down beside the rugby club.

    Helen: Oh, I didn't know he had moved. I was just going to call to him because he left his iPod at my house last week. How do you get to Collins Road from here?

    John: You just turn left at the roundabout at Morgan's pub. That's where the big fight happened last week and bouncers had to break it up. A few of the windows were smashed.

    Helen: Oh, I heard about that yesterday.

    John: Yeah. Anyway, you go along the road there and then up the hill. At the top of the hill you take a left. Mary Wilson lives there. You know the one who wears all the jewellery and the make up?

    Helen: Oh yeah, she was in my class in primary school. I haven't seen her in years though. So then I go…?

    John: So then you go straight on to where the road forks and you take a right. There are nice little cottages there, but they've been talking about knocking it all and building a new cinema. It's right beside where the rugby club is. Kevin lives at number eight along that row.

(a) Why is Helen planning to go to Kevin's house?
_____
_____
_____

(b) What happened at Morgan's pub last week?
_____
_____
_____

(c) What do you know about Mary Wilson?
_____
_____
_____

(d) What is going to be developed instead of the cottages?
_____
_____
_____

(e) In your own words, explain how you get from the shopping centre to Kevin's house.
_____
_____
_____

(f) Do you think John's directions were difficult to follow? Why?
_____
_____
_____

3. Imagine that you are giving directions to a visitor to your school. How would he or she get from the school to the nearest church?
_____
_____
_____
_____

4. Below is a set of instructions for drawing a picture. Follow the instructions and then draw the picture in the box provided. Read each instruction carefully before you begin.

1. Draw a circle, about 1 inch in diameter at the left-hand side of the box. Make sure it touches the bottom of the box.
2. Draw a second circle of the same size, approximately an inch away to the right, ensuring that it also touches the bottom of the page.
3. Put the tip of your pen into the centre of the circle on the left.
4. From that point, drawing towards the right, draw an equilateral triangle, pointing upwards, the base of which is about 1 inch in length.
5. Put your pen on the top point of the triangle. Draw a second equilateral triangle of equal size, pointing downwards. The two triangles should have a side in common.
6. The two triangles together should look like a parallelogram.
7. Put the tip of your pen on the point of the parallelogram furthest to the right.
8. Draw a diagonal line from that point to the centre of the second circle.
9. Above the peak of the first triangle you drew, draw a small oval on its side, about the size of a peanut.
10. Above the right-hand point of the parallelogram, draw a line straight upwards, about 1 cm high.
11. Put your pen on the topmost point of the line and draw a short horizontal line to the left, about 1 cm in length.

Note: *An equilateral triangle is one where all the sides are equal in length.*

(a) What is this a picture of?

_____

_____

(b) From looking at your picture, do you think you followed the instructions properly? Where did you go wrong? Where might others have gone wrong?

_____
_____

(c) What was the most difficult thing about drawing this picture? Why?

_____
_____

(d) Do you think these instructions were clear? Why? Why not?

_____
_____

(e) In what situations might you need to follow complicated instructions like these?

_____
_____
_____

PRACTICAL EXERCISE!

Why not try this class game? Draw a simple picture or shape in the box below. Don't let any other student see it. When it's your turn, give clear instructions to the other students so that they can draw the picture themselves. How well will *you* do? How well will they do? ☺

CHAPTER 3 Telephone Techniques

1. Look at the first few pages of your local telephone directory and identify area codes for the following regions:

    (a) Dublin

    (b) Castletownbere

    (c) Gort

    (d) Navan

    (e) Waterford

2. Find the international dialling code for each of these countries:

    (a) Ireland

    (b) Britain

    (c) U.S.A.

    (d) Australia

    (e) Canada

3. If your friend in Britain wanted to call your mobile here in Ireland, what number would he/she have to dial in order to reach you?

    Write out the number in full and remember: *the first '0' of your number should be dropped after adding the Irish international code.*

    _____

4. List three services provided by Eircom.

    (a) _____

    (b) _____

    (c) _____

5. Explain why each of the following factors is important when making a phone call.

(a) Identification of the caller

(b) Clarity of communication

(c) Tone of voice

(d) Timing of call

(e) Appropriate closure (give an example)

6.

CD - Track 3

Listen to the telephone conversation in Track 3 of the CD. Write down the message that should be taken for this call.

Message

Date: _____ Time: _____ Message For: _____
Caller's Name and tel. no: _____
MESSAGE:

Message Taken by: _____

7.

CD - Track 4

Listen to Track 4 on the CD and write the appropriate telephone message in the box below.

Message

Date: _____ Time: _____ Message For: _____
Caller's Name and tel. no: _____
MESSAGE:

Message Taken by: _____

8. CD - Track 5

Listen to Track 5 on the CD and answer the questions below.

(a) What was wrong with the telephonist's greeting on the phone?

_____

_____

_____

(b) What information did the telephonist fail to get, in order to pass on an appropriate message?

_____

_____

_____

(c) What was wrong with the way the telephonist ended the conversation?

_____

_____

_____

(d) Why do you think the telephonist's supervisor might be angry?

_____

_____

_____

9. Fill in the blanks below.

When answering the phone, it is very important to be p_____. If a customer has an enquiry, try to be as h_____ as you can. Speak c_____ and s_____. If a customer has a complaint, stay c_____ and never raise your v_____. Take an appropriate m_____ and include the c_____ number. When you are at work, only ever make b_____ calls. If your friend rings you at work, keep the call b_____ and return calls to friends during your b_____ on your own m_____ and not on a w_____ phone.

10. List three advantages and three disadvantages of mobile phones.

ADVANTAGES	DISADVANTAGES
(i) _____	(i) _____
(ii) _____	(ii) _____
(iii) _____	(iii) _____

11. Sometimes people have to deal with difficult calls. What tips would you give a telephonist for dealing with an angry customer?

_____
_____
_____
_____
_____

12. Imagine Philip ordered a product from the UK. It took two weeks longer than expected to arrive, and when it did arrive, it was the wrong item. Philip decides to ring the company to complain. What advice would you give to Philip so that he can express his annoyance without being confrontational?

_____
_____
_____
_____
_____

13. Resolving Conflict

Two students should role play the conversation below. In class, discuss the causes of the conflict and the ways that it could have been avoided.

> *Kevin bumps into Ben in the corridor and causes Ben to drop the papers he is carrying.*
>
> **Kevin:** Oh sorry, I didn't see you!
>
> **Ben:** Oh for God's sake, will you watch where you're going?!
>
> **Kevin:** (*getting annoyed*) Will you relax? It was just an accident!
>
> **Ben:** Relax? You barged straight into me! (*Ben picks up his things from the floor.*)
>
> **Kevin:** (*Helping Ben to pick up his things.*) I didn't see you…It's hardly a big deal…
>
> **Ben:** Not a big deal? Look at this mess! Or are you blind as well as stupid?!
>
> **Kevin:** Well, if that's your attitude, pick them up yourself! (*Kevin throws down what he had picked up and marches off.*)

(a) In your opinion, what starts the conflict between Kevin and Ben?

_____
_____
_____
_____

(b) How could Kevin have prevented the conflict from escalating?

_____
_____
_____
_____

(c) How could Ben have expressed his frustration without becoming angry?

_____
_____
_____
_____

(d) Describe a confrontation that you were involved in. How could you have prevented the conflict from escalating?

_____
_____
_____
_____
_____

PRACTICAL EXERCISE!

Using a Dictaphone (tape recorder) practise leaving messages on an answering machine. Remember to leave your name and number and the reason why you are calling! ☺

CHAPTER 4 Writing a Report

1. Writing a report involves doing **research**. What is meant by the term *research*?

   _____
   _____
   _____

2. List and briefly explain three situations where you may have to do some research.

   (a) _____
   _____
   _____

   (b) _____
   _____
   _____

   (c) _____
   _____
   _____

3. What kinds of research can be carried out using the following?

   (a) Local libraries
   _____
   _____

   (b) Art galleries
   _____
   _____

   (c) Museums
   _____
   _____

   (d) Interpretive centres
   _____
   _____

4. List two advantages and two disadvantages of interviews as a source of information.

ADVANTAGES

(i) _____

_____

_____

(ii) _____

_____

_____

DISADVANTAGES

(i) _____

_____

_____

(ii) _____

_____

_____

5. (a) What is meant by the term 'vox pop'?

_____

_____

(b) List three advantages and three disadvantages of a vox pop.

ADVANTAGES

(i) _____

_____

_____

(ii) _____

_____

_____

(iii) _____

_____

_____

DISADVANTAGES

(i) _____

_____

_____

(ii) _____

_____

_____

(iii) _____

_____

_____

STANDARD ASSIGNMENT

Conduct one of the following: an interview, a vox pop or a piece of research.

Present your findings in a report.

Module 1 – Communication and the Working World

ADVANCED ASSIGNMENT

Write a report using <u>two</u> of the following as sources of information: an interview, a vox pop or a piece of research.

WRITING A REPORT

1. Select a topic for research

    (a) Choose something that interests you. Write the selected topic below.
    _____

    (b) What area of this topic are you going to research?
    _____

    > **Example**
    >
    > The topic chosen is football. The area of research is Alex Ferguson's career as Manchester United Manager.

2. Select a report title

What title will you give to your report? Your title should make clear the topic and the area of research.

> **Example**
>
> Manchester United: 23 Years with Sir Alex

3. Purpose of the report

    (a) Why are you writing this report?
    _____
    _____
    _____

    (b) Who will be reading this report?
    _____
    _____
    _____

4. Gathering information

    (a) Information can be gathered using various sources, such as vox pop, interview, personal observation, internet, library, etc.

    List three sources you intend to use in gathering information for your report, explaining why you chose each one.

    (i) _____

    (ii) _____

    (iii) _____

    (b) Write out the *details* of each source, i.e. names of websites, names and authors of books, list of questions for a vox pop, etc.

    _____

5. Findings

    (a) What are the main findings of your report? Present your findings in a logical and impersonal style.

    (i) _____

    (ii) _____

    (iii) _____

(iv) _____
_____
_____

6. Conclusions

(a) What is your opinion on your findings?

_____
_____
_____
_____

Sample Report

Title: Manchester United: 23 Years with Sir Alex

Purpose: Manchester United is one of the most popular teams in English soccer and is an undeniably fascinating club. With 23 years in charge at Manchester United, Sir Alex Ferguson is the second-longest serving manager in the club's history. He is truly an inspiration for our age.

Findings: Ferguson became manager at Old Trafford on 6 November 1986. In the early days, he had concerns about some of the players, especially about their levels of fitness. He felt that many players were drinking too much. Ferguson worked really hard to bring discipline to the team and this helped them to climb the table to eleventh place that season.

The next season Ferguson signed many new players who were expected to boost the club. However, they were disappointed when they finished in eleventh place again. Ferguson continued to work hard with his team and in 1990–91 they had some success and finished sixth. More success came in 1994. Ferguson had players who were worth millions and Eric Cantona was the top scorer, despite being sent off twice!

In 1998–99, to everyone's delight, the club won the treble: Premier League title, FA Cup and the Champions League. Their success has continued right into the twenty-first century. On 11 May 2008 Ferguson successfully brought his team to a tenth Premier League title.

Conclusions: Ferguson's success with Manchester United continues. They are the most thrilling team to watch and from the many games I have attended over the years, they have never let me down! Although, I often wonder where Manchester United would be today if it weren't for the hard work, discipline and foresight of the great Sir Alex Ferguson.

WRITING YOUR OWN REPORT

STANDARD ASSIGNMENT

Visit an interesting place with your class, e.g. library, cinema, theatre, heritage centre, interpretive centre, museum, art gallery, etc. Using the tips in this chapter and the template below, write a report on your visit.

Title: _____

Purpose: _____

_____

_____

_____

_____

Findings: _____

_____

_____

_____

_____

_____

_____

_____

_____

_____

Conclusions: _____

_____

_____

_____

_____

_____

_____

_____

INCORPORATING I.T.

Type your report using Microsoft Word or a similar program. Create a suitable banner headline and include images using Clipart or relevant photos from the Internet. ☺

PRACTICAL EXERCISE!

SOAPBOX!

Present your report to the rest of the class. You could make a PowerPoint presentation. Listen to each report given and decide who would make the best TV reporter. ☺

CHAPTER 5: Writing a Review

1. A review is a critical evaluation of something, e.g. a play or a novel. List some other things that can be reviewed.

    (a) _____

    (b) _____

    (c) _____

    (d) _____

    (e) _____

    (f) _____

2. What is the main purpose of a review?

    _____
    _____
    _____

3. What sort of information would you expect a review to provide?

    _____
    _____
    _____

4. What information would you like to be left out of a review? Why?

    _____
    _____
    _____

5. In which magazines or newspapers would you expect to read the following reviews?

    (a) Film _____
    _____

    (b) Restaurant _____
    _____

    (c) Music album _____
    _____

    (d) Live performance _____
    _____

(e) Novel _____

_____

(f) TV programme _____

_____

6. Read the following review and answer the questions that follow.

Alice in Wonderland

Cert	PG
Director	Tim Burton
Starring	Johnny Depp, Mia Wasikowska, Helena Bonham Carter, Anne Hathaway, Stephen Fry, Matt Lucas, Crispin Glover

The Plot

The original *Alice in Wonderland* by Lewis Carroll is a fantastic, eccentric Victorian tale and, as such, it is no surprise that it caught the attention of Tim Burton. Burton's name has become synonymous with the unconventional in the film world. Following acclaimed films such as *Edward Scissorhands* and *Charlie and the Chocolate Factory*, Burton has dived into a wonderland of nonsensical rhymes and crazy characters.

Alice, played by Mia Wasikowska, is both curious and rebellious. Under pressure to accept a marriage proposal from the rather repulsive Hamish, Alice flees the scene, only to fall down a rabbit hole where she meets an array of marvellous characters. Johnny Depp is truly on form in his portrayal of the Mad Hatter who befriends Alice. The best performance of all comes from Bonham Carter as the Red Queen. While at times she is outlandishly cruel in her screams for beheading, she also displays child-like behaviour; in many ways her neediness evokes our pity.

On the other hand, the real disappointment in this film is the portrayal by Anne Hathaway of the White Queen. She becomes almost a caricature and throughout has the most irritating way of holding her hands! The scenes with Hathaway become something of an annoyance and tend to let down the rest of the film.

Overall it is a film worth seeing. If you are already a Burton fan, this film won't disappoint. Die-hard *Alice in Wonderland* fans might feel a little let down by the fact that it doesn't stick rigidly to the original book, but for the rest of us, it's a colourful, light-hearted giggle for all the family!

Star Rating
✱ ✱ ✱

(a) What is being reviewed?

(b) Summarise the plot of the film.

(c) List some of the film's good points.

(d) List some of the film's bad points.

(e) To what genre does this film belong?

(f) From your reading of this review, would you be interested in seeing this film? Why? Why not?

7. Read the review below and answer the questions that follow.

Robbie Williams

Reality Killed the Video Star

Having been absent from the music world for three long years, Robbie Williams is back with his eighth studio album. His last album, *Rudebox,* was not acclaimed by critics and many believe it is the reason he slunk away from the limelight.

However, Williams has re-established himself on the music circuit with the help of the gifted Trevor Horn; and together they make quite a team! With less emphasis on the electrical music and beats used in previous albums, *Reality Killed the Video Star* lets us enjoy proper orchestral music.

'Deceptacon' is clearly the most ambitious song on the album, so warm and comforting that it certainly won't disappoint! A close second is 'Won't Do That', a brassy pop song that should prove to be a popular sing-along in stadiums and is surely in line for release as a single. The album opens with 'Morning Sun', which sounds like a depressed Beatles song, and while it may not be upbeat, it really is a return to what Williams does best.

The weakest song on the album is 'Bodies', which seems to be a little frenzied and disjointed, much like Williams himself at his recent comeback performance on *The X-Factor*. While elements of the song will have techno fans racing for the dance floor, the rest is old-fashioned pop.

There really is a lot packed into this album and the more you listen to it the more you become hooked. It's a step away from his usual techno and electrical tricks and a move back into the musicality of instruments, which many fans have been missing. This is an album that proves that Robbie Williams is most definitely back with a bang!

Star Rating
✶ ✶ ✶ ✶

(a) What is being reviewed?

_____

(b) How many albums has Robbie Williams released to date?

_____

(c) To what genre of music does this album belong?

_____

(d) List two positive aspects of this album.

    (i) _____

_____

(ii) _____

(e) From reading this review, would you be interested in buying this Robbie Williams album? Why? Why not? Refer to the review in your answer.

_____

_____

_____

_____

LESSON BOX!

A review must answer **three** basic questions:

1. What is being reviewed?

You must answer the 'five w's and one h':

- Who?
- What?
- Where?
- When?
- Why?
- How?

For a novel, play, film, etc. this would include: who wrote it, the title, a brief outline of the plot, the characters, its setting, etc. If the subject being reviewed is a CD album or live performance, you must explain: who was involved, the venue, etc.

It is important that you answer these basic questions so that the reader knows all the details of the subject being reviewed.

2. What method is used?

If this is a play, novel or film, describing the method used would include a mention of the genre. Describe *how* the artist attempted to tell the story (from whose point of view, etc.). You may also describe the main character and the situation he/she faces. If you are reviewing a CD or live performance, describe the genre of music. What style of music is it? What is distinctive about the subject matter?

3. What is your personal opinion?

What are the good points about the subject being reviewed? What worked? Did the artist succeed in creating what he intended? What aspect really appealed to you?

What are the negative points about the subject being reviewed? Remember, a review is seldom completely negative. There is no need to repeat phrases like 'I think' or 'in my opinion', as the reader will already grasp your opinion.

DRAMA

Read the extract below and answer the questions that follow.

Father Ted
'The Passion of Saint Tibulus'

SCENE 1 (PAROCHIAL HOUSE)

Through the rain-streaked window of the Parochial House, we see Father Dougal McGuire, a young innocent-looking priest, staring out at the night. Occasionally his face is illuminated by flashes of lightning. From the noise, we can assume that the rain is pummelling the earth.

We then see Father Ted Crilly sitting at a table with a handsome, black-haired priest. This is Father Josẽ Hernandez, a Cuban. Whenever he speaks, his dialogue is dubbed (no one comments on this). His 'voice' is very deep and smooth; he sounds like a real lady-killer. The two priests are seated around a Cluedo board. They are drinking cups of tea. A large brown candle burns in the centre of the table. Father Jack Hackett, an elderly man whom we can't see clearly as yet, watches television in another part of the room. Cut to Dougal, who is still watching the torrential rain. We see more lightning and hear more thunder.

Dougal: Looks like rain, Ted.

Ted raises his eyes heavenward when he hears this.

Ted: Dougal, come on. It's your turn.

Dougal walks over and assumes his place at the table. He rolls some dice. Ted smiles at Hernandez.

Ted: (brightly) I must say, Father Hernandez, it's been wonderful having you over. But I expect you're getting a bit homesick for Cuba by now.

Josẽ: (dubbed) Si. Mi pais es muy hermoso.

   [Yes. My country is very beautiful.]

   Pero, Ted, usted es un hombre muy afortunado. En Craggy Island tiene usted dos Buenos amigos, el Padre Dougal.

   [But Ted, you have a great life here on Craggy Island. You have two good friends, Father Dougal…]

Shot of Dougal choking on something. He gags for a while and then takes one of the Cluedo pieces out of his mouth and looks at it quizzically.

   …Y claro, el Padre Jack.

   […And of course, Father Jack.]

We see Father Jack's face for the first time. We hear the sound of flies buzzing. His mouth hangs open and a thin line of drool hangs from his mouth. His teeth are yellow.

Mrs. Doyle enters with more tea.

Ted: Yes…yes, it's…it's great here. Although, I must say, sometimes I miss the noise and the lights and the…you know, the whole buzz of the big city.

José: Usted estaba en Wexford, verdad?

[You were in Wexford, weren't you?]

Ted: I was, yes. But, you know, Craggy Island has its charms. The west part of the island was beautiful. Until it drifted off, of course.

José: Se desprendio?

[Drifted off?]

Ted: Yes. There was a bit of a storm and it came loose. Now, of course, we don't have a west side. It's just north, south and east. But while it was there it was lovely.

José: Sabe usted Ted…su ama de llaves es una mujer muy hermosa.

[You know, Ted, your housekeeper is a very beautiful woman.]

He smiles at Mrs. Doyle. She doesn't know how to deal with this, and makes a hasty exit.

José: En ocasiones esto del celibate es muy duro para un hombre…je, je, je…

[Sometimes, this celibacy is hard for a man…heh, heh…]

Ted: Oh well…you have to take the rough with the smooth, I suppose. Bishop Brennan springs to mind.

José: Ah si…?

[Oh yes…?]

Ted: Yes, Bishop Brennan. He's our…kind of boss, I suppose. He's the one who thought Dougal and Father Jack would be better off working here…on an island with, you know…a very small population. Anyway, the rumour is that his housekeeper caught him once, ah, 'in delicto flagrante'. They say, ah…they say the union was 'blessed' if you know what I mean.

José: No!...Nino o nina?

[No!...boy or girl?]

Ted: A boy, I think. Lives in America now, or so goes the rumour anyway!

Dougal: Was it…Colonel Mustard…in the kitchen…with the candlestick?

Ted: What?

Dougal: Colonel Mustard, in the kitchen with the candlestick?

Ted: But you have Colonel Mustard! You showed him to me earlier! How could it be Colonel Mustard if you have Colonel Mustard?!!

Slight pause…

Dougal: Ohhh, right…

Ted: Father Hernandez, your go…

> **José:** Si…Creo que fue ei Reverendo Green…con el cuchillo…en la estancia.
> [Yes…I think it was Reverend Green, with the knife, in the drawing room.]
>
> **Ted:** Those Protestants! Up to no good as usual!
>
> *Everyone laughs softly…*

1. Who are the main characters involved in this drama?

2. Why are they on Craggy Island?

3. Describe Dougal's character. Refer to the text in your answer.

4. Describe three areas of the text that you found funny.

   (a)

   (b)

   (c)

5. Going by this extract, which character do you think is the best? Why?
   _____
   _____
   _____

6. To what genre does this drama belong?
   _____
   _____
   _____

7. From your reading of the text, do you think you would like to read more of this drama? Why? Why not?
   _____
   _____
   _____

8. What do you think will happen in the next scene of this text? Why?
   _____
   _____
   _____
   _____

Read the extract below and answer the questions that follow.

SCENE 5 (PAROCHIAL HOUSE)

Dougal is down on all fours, messing around with the VCR. Ted is cleaning up the room.

Ted: C'mon, Dougal. The Bishop'll be here any minute.

Dougal: Oh, right.

Ted: Now, do you remember what I told you?

Dougal: Eh…

Ted: It's very simple. On no account mention what we were talking about last night.

Dougal: Right. (*Pause*) What were we talking about last night?

Ted: You know…the rumours about the Bishop's little mistake.

Dougal: Right. (*Pause*). What mistake was that, Ted?

Ted: His son. His son in America.

Dougal: Oh, yes. (*Pause*). He has a son in America?

Ted: Yes! Well, so they say…

Dougal: Right, OK. (*Pause*). That's news to me, Ted.

Ted: We were talking about it last night, Dougal! To Father Hernandez.

Dougal: Who? Oh, right! The Cuban lad…

Ted: But you remember now…not a word about the son…

Dougal: Oh, right!

Ted: …Just…forget about all that, all right? Forget about it. Don't say a word. Have you got that?

Dougal: I have, Ted.

Ted: I don't want you saying anything stupid.

Dougal: The lights are on, but there's nobody home, Ted.

Ted: Are you sure?

Dougal: I am indeed, Ted. Don't worry about that at all.

Ted: Grand. Alright. I think that's everything.

He notices that Jack's hair is a little awry. He approaches him gingerly, producing a comb as he does so.

Ted: …Father, do you think I could…?

It's just for the Bishop. We should have you looking your best…

Maybe it's fine. We'll leave it as it is. Let it settle.

Mrs. Doyle enters.

Mrs. Doyle: Father Crilly, Bishop Brennan is here.

Ted: Hell's bells! Right…Show him in. (*to Dougal*) Dougal, please remember, whatever you do, not a word about the son. Honestly, this is the most important thing I'll ever ask you to do. Don't say a word.

Dougal: There's no danger of that whatsoever, Ted.

Ted: OK.

Mrs. Doyle brings in the Bishop. He is about fifty and very stern-faced. He has a large leather carrier bag.

Ted: Ah hello, Bishop Brennan. Are you well?

The bishop barely acknowledges their presence. Jack, in turn, is oblivious to the Bishop's arrival. Dougal smiles happily.

Ted: Your Eminence, sit down there beside Father Dougal. Mrs. Doyle, could you make some tea for us?

Mrs. Doyle: Certainly, Father.

The Bishop sits beside Dougal. Ted sits down in a chair opposite them both. Dougal watches the Bishop closely. We hear a clock ticking. Dougal clears his throat ominously. There is a very, very long pause.

Dougal: How's the son?

The bishop bristles visibly.

Bishop: What?

Ted: (*panicking*) The Son of God. How is the Son of God? Everything well in the world of religion?

Bishop: What? The world of religion? What are you talking about, Crilly?

Ted: You know…ah…Mrs. Doyle! Is that tea ready?! Ha, ha!

Mrs. Doyle enters, carrying a tray.

Mrs. Doyle: Here I am! Here I am!...Ah, isn't this grand?

She hands a cup to the Bishop. He puts his hand out to stop her.

Bishop: I'm fine, thank you, Mrs. Doyle.

Mrs. Doyle: Will you not have a cup of tea, Bishop Brennan?

Bishop: No, no, I'm not staying long. I just want to get right to the point and get the hell out of here.

Mrs. Doyle: Are you sure you won't have a cup?

Bishop: Certain, thank you. *(to Ted)* Now, I –

Mrs. Doyle: Go on, have a cup.

Bishop: I won't, thanks.

Mrs. Doyle: Everyone else is having a cup. Will you not have one yourself?

Bishop: No, I don't have time. Crilly, I –

Mrs. Doyle: You'll feel left out. You'll be Bishop Piggy in the Middle.

Bishop: I'm fine. I'm fine.

Mrs. Doyle: You sure you won't have a cup? Just a drop?

Bishop: No!...

Mrs. Doyle: *(sings softly)* Bishop Piggy in the Middle…

Ted leans over.

Ted: *(whispers)* Actually, Your Eminence, just say Yes. It's quicker, believe me.

Bishop: All right, then.

Mrs. Doyle: *(pleased)* Grand!

She gives him the tea and leaves. The Bishop addresses the three priests.

Bishop: Well, I hope you're not doing too much damage here. Jack, are you behaving yourself?

Jack is smoking a fag. He blows out some smoke contemptuously.

Jack: *(under his breath)*…Feck off!

Bishop: What did you say?

Ted: Ha, ha! Anyway, Your Eminence, what brings you to the island? Are you thinking of letting us head back to our old parishes?

Bishop: Fat chance! You're here until I tell you otherwise. Do you think I'd let Jack back into a normal parish after what he did in Athlone? How do you think I felt when I had to explain that to Cardinal Daly?

Ted: Well, yes…surely I'm all right…

Bishop: No, no. You're here until every penny of that money is accounted for.

Ted: I told you, that money was just resting in my account until…

Bishop: Enough!

Ted: I don't know where it went!

Bishop: Crilly, I won't tell you again. And as for this…cabbage…*(Dougal looks very uncomfortable. Ted goes very quiet.)*…The mere idea of letting him back into the real world after The Blackrock Incident.

Ted: (*quietly*) Yes, that was…unfortunate.

Bishop: The amount of lives irreparably damaged…The tourist industry shattered in a single blow…My God, do you know how many strings I had to pull to stop the Vatican getting involved?

Jack chuckles to himself. Dougal is ashen-faced.

Bishop: I don't even want to talk about it. I just want to get this film thing over with.

Ted: Film? What film?

Bishop: This…whatever it's called…film. *The Passion of Saint Tibulus*. His holiness banned it, but because of some loophole the bloody thing's being shown here on this godforsaken hellhole.

Dougal: Oh, yes, that's right. Is it any good, do you know?

Bishop: I don't care if it's any good or not! All I know is that we have to be seen to be making a stand against it. That's where you and Larry and Moe come in.

Ted: What do you mean?

Bishop: I know that normally you wouldn't be able to organise a nun-shoot in a nunnery, but it's up to you to make the Church's position clear. Make some kind of protest. Even you should be able to manage that.

Dougal: Thanks very much.

Bishop: This is very important. Don't make a balls of it. I'll be in touch.

Ted: Ah…ah, Your Eminence? This isn't really my area.

Bishop: Nothing's your area, Crilly. You don't have an area! Unless it's a kind of play area with sandcastles and buckets and spades. Just do what you're told, all right?

He leaves the room, slamming the door. There is a quiet pause.

Dougal: Bye, then!

Channel 4, *Father Ted*, Series 1

1. What warning does Ted give Dougal at the beginning of this scene?

   _____
   _____

2. Ted is quite nervous about Bishop Brennan's visit. What evidence from the text is there to support this statement?

   _____
   _____
   _____
   _____
   _____

3. Describe Bishop Brennan. What kind of person is he?

   _____
   _____
   _____
   _____
   _____

4. Why has he come to visit the three priests on the island?

   _____
   _____
   _____

5. What parts of this scene did you find humorous? Explain your answer.

   _____
   _____
   _____
   _____

6. From reading this extract, would you be interested in reading further scenes? Why? Why not?

   _____
   _____
   _____
   _____
   _____

WRITING YOUR REVIEW

STANDARD ASSIGNMENT

Write or record your review of <u>one</u> of the following: a short story, a novel (or extract), a drama (or extract), a poem or a song.

Write a review of a drama (perhaps these extracts from *Father Ted*). Remember to answer the <u>three</u> basic questions outlined in the Lesson Box on page 30 of this chapter.

Beat! LCA English Assignments Workbook

INCORPORATING I.T.

Type your review using Microsoft Word or a similar program. ☺

PRACTICAL EXERCISE!

Jonathan Ross used to present *The Film Programme,* a film review show on BBC One. See if you can find a clip of his reviews on YouTube.

Imagine you are Jonathan Ross. You can present your review to your class as he would! Practise performing your review using a tape recorder. ☺

ADVANCED ASSIGNMENT

Select a novel to read with your class. Write a review of the novel for publication in a school magazine. Type your review using Microsoft Word or a similar program.

CHAPTER 6 — Curriculum Vitae and Letter Writing Skills

1. List three advantages and three disadvantages of writing letters.

   ADVANTAGES
   (i) _____
   _____
   _____
   (ii) _____
   _____
   _____
   (iii) _____
   _____
   _____

   DISADVANTAGES
   (i) _____
   _____
   _____
   (ii) _____
   _____
   _____
   (iii) _____
   _____
   _____

2. Describe a situation where you would use the following.

   (a) Personal letter

   _____
   _____
   _____
   _____

   (b) Business letter

   _____
   _____
   _____
   _____

41

(c) Formal letter

_____
_____
_____
_____

(d) Covering letter

_____
_____
_____
_____

(e) Letter of complaint

_____
_____
_____
_____

3. Where in a letter do you write *your* address?

_____
_____
_____

4. Sometimes a letter contains a second address on the left-hand side of the page. What is this address for?

_____
_____
_____

5. Where do you put the date on a letter?

_____
_____
_____

Module 1 – Communication and the Working World

6. In which situation would you sign off as follows?

   (a) Yours sincerely

   _____
   _____

   (b) Yours faithfully

   _____
   _____

   (c) Regards

   _____
   _____

   (d) See you soon

   _____
   _____

7. Examine the list of phrases below and decide which are formal and which are informal. Write each phrase in the appropriate column.

   - Hi, John
   - See you later
   - Yours faithfully
   - Dear Sir
   - I am writing to request
   - Thanks for the invitation
   - I enclose my CV
   - Tell them all I said hello

FORMAL	INFORMAL

43

PERSONAL LETTERS

STANDARD ASSIGNMENT

Prepare a personal letter using a computer.

8. You have been invited to your friend's twenty-first birthday party next week. However, you have to work that night and can't attend. Using a computer, write a letter to your friend, explaining the situation and expressing your disappointment.

_____
_____
_____
_____
/   /20

Dear _____ ,

I got the invitation to your twenty-first party in the post yesterday _____

Module 1 – Communication and the Working World

BUSINESS LETTERS

STANDARD ASSIGNMENT

Prepare a business letter using I.T.

9. Write a letter to a local business, asking for sponsorship for an event you are organising in your school. In your letter you must:

   - describe the event and explain why you are staging it;
   - state how sponsorship would be helpful to your school;
   - explain how sponsoring the event might be helpful for the business;
   - use the appropriate layout and language.

_____
_____
_____
_____
          /   /20

_____
_____
_____
_____

                    Re: _____

Dear _____ ,

I am writing to you _____
_____
_____
_____
_____

Looking forward to hearing from you

Yours _____
_____

LETTERS OF COMPLAINT AND REQUEST

10. (a) In what situation might you write a letter of complaint?

(b) Why do you think it is important to complain in writing?

(c) Why would you send a copy of a receipt rather than the original?

(d) Why is it important not to be rude in a letter of complaint, even if you are angry?

(e) What details should you put in the letter if you are complaining about a product that you purchased?

-
-
-

(f) In what situations might you write a letter of request?

(g) List three ways in which a letter of request differs from a letter of complaint.

-
-
-

Module 1 – Communication and the Working World

> **PRACTICAL EXERCISE!**
>
> Why not send a letter to a local business, asking if you can do your work placement with them? Make sure you type your letter and address the envelope appropriately. ☺

11. Write a letter to an entrepreneur in your area, asking him/her to give a talk in your school or to provide you with information on how to set up a business.

_____
_____
_____
_____

___/___/20

_____
_____
_____
_____

Re: _____

Dear _____ ,

I am writing to you _____
_____
_____
_____
_____
_____
_____
_____

Looking forward to hearing from you

Yours _____

_____

47

CURRICULUM VITAE

12. List three purposes of a CV.

(i) _____

(ii) _____

(iii) _____

ADVANCED ASSIGNMENT

Prepare a covering letter.

13. This advertisement appears in your local newspaper:

> Student required for summer work in busy seaside hotel.
> Apply in writing to: **The Manager, Seaview Hotel, Galway.**

Using a computer, write the covering letter that would form part of your application for this job.

_____
_____
_____
_____

____ / ____ /20

_____

_____

_____

_____

Dear _____ ,

I refer to your advertisement in _____

_____

_____

_____

_____

_____

_____

_____

_____

_____

Yours _____

ADVANCED ASSIGNMENT

Prepare a CV.

14. Fill out this CV template. Then create your own version, using a computer.

CURRICULUM VITAE

PERSONAL DETAILS

Name _____

Address _____

_____

_____

Telephone no. _____

Date and place of birth _____/_____/_____

EDUCATIONAL DETAILS

_____ to present _____

(secondary) _____

_____ (year) _____

(primary) _____

Junior Certificate Results

SUBJECT	RESULT
_____	_____
_____	_____
_____	_____
_____	_____
_____	_____
_____	_____
_____	_____
_____	_____

INTERESTS, HOBBIES AND ACHIEVEMENTS

- _____
  _____

- _____
  _____

- _____
  _____

WORK EXPERIENCE

1. Date _____

Place of work _____

Job title _____

Duties undertaken _____

2. Date _____

Place of work _____

Job title _____

Duties undertaken _____

REFERENCES

1. Name _____

Address _____
_____

Telephone No. _____

2. Name _____

Address _____
_____

Telephone No. _____

15. Fill out the following job application form.

EMPLOYMENT APPLICATION

Name _____ Date of birth _____

Address _____

_____ Male ☐   Female ☐

EDUCATION

School	Dates	Examination results
_____	_____	_____
_____	_____	_____
_____	_____	_____
_____	_____	_____

WORK EXPERIENCE

Employer	Duties undertaken	Duration
_____	_____	_____
_____	_____	_____
_____	_____	_____
_____	_____	_____

HOBBIES

_____

_____

_____

SPECIAL SKILLS (e.g. woodwork, metalwork, art, cooking, etc.) _____

_____

WOULD YOU EXPERIENCE DIFFICULTY WITH ANY OF THE FOLLOWING?
(Tick where appropriate)

Heavy lifting ☐   Outdoor work ☐   Allergies ☐   Odours (paints/glues) ☐   Other ☐

If you ticked 'other', please give details: _____
_____

HAVE YOU EVER SUFFERED FROM ANY SERIOUS ILLNESS?   Yes ☐   No ☐

If yes, please give details: _____
_____

DO YOU HOLD A CURRENT DRIVING LICENCE?   Yes ☐   No ☐

HOW SOON ARE YOU AVAILABLE FOR WORK? _____
_____

PLEASE GIVE CONTACT DETAILS OF REFEREES (NOT RELATIVES):

1. Name _____

   Address _____

   _____

   Telephone No. _____

2. Name _____

   Address _____

   _____

   Telephone No. _____

If you are employed at present, one of your references <u>must</u> come from your present employer.

Signature of Applicant _____   Date _____

FOR OFFICE USE ONLY   Assignment _____   Date _____

                       Status change _____   Date _____

End of Module Checklist:
Communication and the Working World

At the end of this module, you should have a copy of **each** of the following in your folder to ensure you gain full credits. It is important that you use I.T. wherever possible.

1. A typed **REPORT** on a particular topic, using research sources such as 'vox pop', interview, etc.

2. A typed **REPORT** on your visit to a library, cinema, theatre, heritage centre, interpretive centre, museum or art gallery.

3. A typed **REVIEW** of a short story, novel, drama, poem or song.

4. A typed **PERSONAL LETTER**.

5. A typed **BUSINESS LETTER**.

6. Your up-to-date **CURRICULUM VITAE**.

7. A **COVERING LETTER** of application to be sent with your CV.

Module TWO

Communication and Enterprise

CHAPTER 7 Introduction to Enterprise

1. Explain the following business terms.

    (a) Meeting

    (b) Chairperson

    (c) Secretary

    (d) Treasurer

    (e) Agenda

    (f) Minutes

    (g) Proposal

(h) Lodgment

_____
_____
_____

(i) Withdrawal

_____
_____
_____

(j) Prototype

_____
_____
_____

(k) Market research

_____
_____
_____

2. Using the words in the box below, complete the following sentences:

employees	managing director	shareholder
market	consumers	profit
research	shares	capital

(a) The person in charge of running a company is the _____.

(b) A person who invests money in a company is called a _____.
They buy _____ in that company.

(c) People who work in a company are called _____.

(d) People who buy a company's products are called _____.

(e) The area where goods are sold is called the _____.

(f) If a company's income is greater than its expenditure, it will make a _____.

(g) The money invested in a company is called _____.

(h) The _____ department is responsible for new ideas and products.

3. Write a brief description of the following terms:

   (a) Shareholder

   (b) Logo

   (c) Projected sales

   (d) Cheque

   (e) Credit

   (f) Quality control

STANDARD ASSIGNMENT

Meet with a self-employed person, an enterprise advisor or a bank/credit union representative. Interview the person and write a report on your findings.

> ✓ **Useful TIP!**
>
> This assignment can also be used as part of your research for a mini-company. Interviewing a self-employed person can give you an important insight into the running of your own business.

4. Invite a self-employed person to speak to your class. After their visit, answer these questions.

(a) Who did you interview?

_____
_____

(b) What is the name of their business?

_____
_____

(c) When did they set it up?

_____
_____

(d) What kind of work does the company do?

_____
_____
_____

(e) How many employees are in the company?

_____
_____

(f) What legal requirements had to be met in order to set up the company?

_____
_____
_____
_____

(g) What kind of experience do you think is necessary to run a successful business?

_____
_____
_____
_____

(h) What, according to your interviewee, are the advantages and disadvantages of running your own business?

ADVANTAGES

- _____
_____
_____
_____

- _____
_____
_____
_____

- _____
_____
_____
_____

DISADVANTAGES

- _____
_____
_____
_____

- _____
_____
_____
_____

- _____
_____
_____
_____

(i) What sources of capital were needed to fund the company in the beginning?

_____
_____
_____

(j) How long did it take before the company started to make a profit?

_____
_____
_____

(k) What kind of research was done before setting up the company?

_____
_____
_____

(l) Where does your interviewee expect the business to be in five years' time?

_____
_____
_____

(m) Would your interviewee change anything about their company? Why?

_____
_____
_____
_____

> ✓ **Useful TIP!**
> Interviewing a credit union or bank representative could help you to decide on funding when you are running your own mini-company in the next chapter! ☺

ADVANCED ASSIGNMENT

5. **Invite a credit union or bank representative to your school. Ask them the following questions and write down their answers.**

(a) Where do you work?

_____
_____
_____

(b) Describe a typical day in your workplace.

_____
_____
_____
_____

(c) What hours do you have to work each day?

_____
_____
_____

(d) What qualifications do you require for this job?

_____
_____
_____

(e) What are the advantages and the disadvantages of your job?

ADVANTAGES	DISADVANTAGES
o _____	o _____
o _____	o _____
o _____	o _____

(f) What services are provided by your bank or credit union?

_____
_____
_____

(g) What services provided by *your* bank are not provided by other saving and lending organisations?

_____
_____
_____

(h) How does a bank or credit union make its money?

_____
_____
_____

(i) What information would a potential client have to present in order to get a loan?

_____
_____
_____

(j) How does a bank or credit union decide on how much a person can borrow?

_____
_____
_____

(k) If a person borrows money for a new business venture, how do you know that the business will succeed?

_____
_____
_____

(l) What do you do if a person cannot repay a loan?

_____
_____
_____

(m) How old do you have to be to open an account in your bank or credit union?

_____
_____
_____

(n) How do you think banking in Ireland will change in the future? What new services can Irish people look forward to?

_____
_____
_____
_____

CHAPTER 8 Advertising

STANDARD ASSIGNMENT

Using this chapter as your guide, complete a short study of aspects of advertising and present a report on your findings.

1. List the various forms of advertising:
   - T_____
   - N_____
   - B_____
   - M_____
   - R_____
   - F_____

2. (a) What is the most expensive form of advertising? Why?

   _____
   _____
   _____

   (b) What is the least expensive form of advertising? Why?

   _____
   _____
   _____

3. The three purposes of advertising are listed below. Give an example of each type of advertisement and briefly explain it.

   (a) To promote a product

   _____
   _____
   _____

   (b) To promote a service

   _____
   _____
   _____

(c) To change a behaviour

4. Explain the following terms.

   (a) Gender stereotyping

   (b) Age stereotyping

   (c) Target audience

5. Advertisers use many techniques to persuade us to buy their product or service:

   - the unfinished comparison;
   - a positive view;
   - a negative view;
   - statistics;
   - endorsement;
   - scare the buyer;
   - promotion;
   - the meaningless promise.

   Match each of the techniques above to an explanation below.

   - Advertisers offer customers free gifts or money off the product for a limited time, e.g. 50% extra free.

   _____

   - Advertisers describe how your life will be improved if you have this product. They use words like 'happy', 'clean', 'easy', 'peaceful' and 'safe'.

   _____

- This technique uses words that worry or scare the buyer into believing they will not be safe or happy until they have a specific product, e.g. 'Would you feel safe in your home without this alarm system?'

  _____

- This technique uses surveys and percentages to show how popular the product or service is, e.g. 'Nine out of ten cats prefer it!'

  _____

- This is when the advertiser makes a claim, but uses wording that renders the claim meaningless, e.g. 'May help with weight loss'.

  _____

- Advertisers make it sound like they are comparing their product to similar products, but leave the comparison unfinished, e.g. 'For a brighter smile!'

  _____

- Sometimes advertisers hire celebrities to help promote their products. They may also use 'experts' to help with promotion, e.g. toothpaste recommended by dentists.

  _____

- Advertisers try to show the customer how unhappy they would be without the product. Advertisements for cleaning products use words like 'greasy', 'germs', 'dark' and 'grimy' to describe kitchens where their product has not been used.

  _____

6. Examine this advertisement and answer the questions that follow.

   (a) What product is being advertised?

   _____

   (b) Who is the target audience? Explain your answer.

   _____

   _____

   _____

   _____

   (c) Where would you expect to find this type of advertisement? Explain your answer.

   _____

   _____

Module 2 – Communication and Enterprise

(d) Describe the illustration in this advertisement. What is its purpose?

_____

_____

(e) In your own words, explain what information is given in the copy (text) of the advertisement.

_____

_____

_____

_____

(f) Look again at the techniques of persuasion used by advertisers. Identify and explain three techniques used in this advertisement.

- _____

    _____

    _____

- _____

    _____

    _____

    _____

- _____

    _____

    _____

(g) What other information do you think should be included in this advertisement? Why?

_____

_____

_____

_____

(h) Would you be interested in buying this product? Explain your answer.

_____

_____

_____

7. Examine this advertisement and answer the questions that follow.

   (a) What is the main purpose of this advertisement?

   _____
   _____
   _____
   _____
   _____

   (b) Who is it aimed at, i.e. who is the target audience? Explain your answer.

   _____
   _____
   _____
   _____
   _____

   (c) Where would you expect to find this advertisement? Explain.

   _____
   _____
   _____

   (d) Describe the illustrations used. What is their purpose?

   _____
   _____
   _____

   (e) What is the caption? What does it mean?

   _____
   _____
   _____
   _____
   _____

(f) Look again at the techniques of persuasion used by advertisers. Identify and explain three techniques used in this advertisement.

- _____
_____
_____
_____

- _____
_____
_____
_____

- _____
_____
_____
_____

(g) Do you think this advertisement is effective? Why? Why not?

_____
_____
_____

(h) If this advertisement was to be made for television, at what time in the programming schedule would you show it? Explain your answer.

_____
_____
_____
_____

(i) Name three other advertisements that attempt to change people's behaviour.

- _____
- _____
- _____

8. Examine this advertisement and answer the questions that follow.

   (a) What is the purpose of this advertisement?

   _____
   _____
   _____
   _____

   (b) Who is the target audience? Explain your answer.

   _____
   _____
   _____
   _____
   _____
   _____

   (c) Where would you expect to find this type of advertisement? Explain your answer.

   _____
   _____
   _____
   _____

   (d) Describe the illustrations used in this advertisement. Do you think they are effective?

   _____
   _____
   _____
   _____

   (e) In your own words, explain what information is given in the copy (text) of the advertisement.

   _____
   _____
   _____
   _____

(f) Look again at the techniques of persuasion used by advertisers. Identify and explain three techniques used in this advertisement.

- _____
_____
_____

- _____
_____
_____

- _____
_____
_____

(g) What other information do you think should be included in this advertisement? Why?

_____
_____
_____
_____

(h) Do you think this advertisement is effective? Why? Why not?

_____
_____
_____
_____

9. Examine the advertisement below, which appeared in the Classifieds section of a daily newspaper. Answer the questions that follow.

> **VOLVO**
> '03 Volvo V70, 7-seater, petrol, manual. Navy blue, beige interior. 92k mls. NCT 01/11. €6,500. Phone 087 1234 5678.

(a) What is the purpose of this advertisement?

_____
_____

(b) Describe the product for sale.

_____
_____
_____

(c) Why does the advertisement use abbreviated English? What benefit would this give to:

- the newspaper?

_____
_____
_____

- the seller?

_____
_____
_____

INCORPORATING I.T.

Design an advertisement for a product of your choice. Your advertisement can take any form: print (poster or flyer), radio (scripted for the school intercom), etc. You could use a computer to design it, or record it using a camcorder or tape recorder. Present your finished work to your class. ☺

PRACTICAL EXERCISE!

Select an advertisement from a newspaper, magazine, radio or television. Prepare a presentation on the advertisement, highlighting its techniques of persuasion and its effectiveness. Use Microsoft PowerPoint or a similar program to assist you in your presentation! ☺

CHAPTER 9 Setting up a Mini-company

This module in Communications and Enterprise is concurrent with the Enterprise 1 Module in Vocational Preparation and Guidance. Students can complete a variety of tasks, including setting up a mini-company. This chapter aims to assist you in setting up a mini-company and offers you a possible layout for your Vocational Preparation and Guidance Task, should you choose this option. It also covers the assignment (with a focus on communications).

STANDARD ASSIGNMENT

Participate in the planning and evaluating of a sales and marketing strategy in an enterprise. Keep notes on your meetings.

Each of the following headings can be used to show the examiner the processes undertaken in completing your task!

1. Brainstorming

> ✓ **Useful TIP!**
> See the end of this chapter for mini-company suggestions.

(a) What practical subjects do you take as part of your Leaving Certificate Applied course?

_____
_____
_____

(b) In these practical classes, what kinds of products could you make to sell?

_____
_____
_____

(c) Which products would be easiest to make?

_____
_____
_____

(d) Which products would be easiest to sell? Why?

_____
_____
_____

(e) Which products would be the cheapest and quickest to produce?

_____
_____
_____

(f) Bearing in mind the questions above, select your business venture by taking a vote in class. What product did you choose to market and sell for your mini-company?

_____
_____
_____

(g) Your company must have a trading name. Brainstorm a list of all possible names. Write the list below:

_____
_____
_____

(h) Take a class vote on each of the possible names. What name did your class choose?

_____
_____
_____

(i) What is the target market for your product?

_____
_____
_____

(j) Now that you have selected a product and a name, you must design a logo. Draw a suitable logo in the box below. Take a class vote to decide on the best logo for your company.

> **INCORPORATING I.T.**
>
> Once your class has decided on their favourite logo, use Microsoft Publisher or a similar program to design it. Give the logo a professional and modern touch!

Sample Brainstorming Session

> In our school, we study lots of different practical subjects, such as woodwork, metalwork, art and home economics. In our class, we made a list of all the products that we could make in each subject. We could make candles in art, as our teacher has taught us how to do that. We could make a wine rack or breadboard in woodwork. We knew how to make key-holders from our metalwork class. We could also make cakes and buns from our home economics class.
>
> We thought that making candles, breadboards and key-holders would take a really long time. Cakes seemed to be the quickest thing to make and we all liked doing that in home economics class. Also, cakes would be cheap to produce and easy to sell to students in school, which was our main market.
>
> We put this idea to vote: sixteen students chose to make cakes; two students voted for setting up a carpentry company to make breadboards and wine racks; and one student voted for candle-making. The vote was carried and our class began our first enterprise: a bakery.
>
> Now our mini-company needed a trading name. Each student came up with an idea and each name was listed on the blackboard. Once every suggestion was on the board, we voted for the most popular. The ideas included '6A Bake Sale', 'Buns in the Oven' and 'Kells Cakes'. 'Kells Cakes' was the most popular choice and that became the name of our mini-company!

2. Aims

Personal aims

(a) List five things you want to learn from setting up this mini-company.

- _____
  _____
  _____
- _____
  _____
  _____
- _____
  _____
  _____

Beat! LCA English Assignments Workbook

○ _____
_____
_____

○ _____
_____
_____

(b) List three skills you would like to improve by doing this task.

○ _____
_____
_____

○ _____
_____
_____

○ _____
_____
_____

Group aims

(c) List three of your group's aims for setting up the mini-company and explain what you can learn from working in a group.

○ _____
_____
_____

○ _____
_____
_____

○ _____
_____
_____

Example of aims

> ### Personal aims
>
> - I want to learn how to set up and run a profitable company.
> - I want to learn how to bake a variety of different cakes and buns from recipes.
> - I want to learn how to advertise a product.
> - I want to find out if I would like to run a business in the future.
> - I want to learn about each of the different roles in a company and how they must all work together.
> - I want to improve my typing skills.
> - I want to improve my communication skills by sitting a mock interview.
> - I want to improve my teamwork skills.
>
> ### Group aims
>
> - We aim to work as a team and co-operate in order to get the job done.
> - We aim to invest money that will benefit the group and to share our profits.
> - We want to learn how important it is that everyone carries out their share of the work to make the company a success.
> - We want to see who would be the best at running a company and who has the best ideas!

3. Research

Interview with a self-employed person

> ✓ **Useful TIP!**
>
> In Chapter 7, you interviewed a self-employed person. Refer to your interview in the research section of this task. You could also interview a bank or credit union representative. What did you learn from them about running a business? ☺

Prototype

This is a sample of one of your products (e.g. make one chocolate cake).

INCORPORATING I.T.

Why not design your packaging using Microsoft Publisher or a similar program? ☺

(a) List three pieces of research that you could undertake to find a suitable recipe, pattern or blueprint for your product.

- _____
- _____
- _____

(b) Write down the recipe or pattern that you followed in order to make your product. Draw any blueprints you used.

_____

(c) How much did your materials cost?

_____
_____

(d) How long did it take to make your product?

_____
_____
_____

(e) How much would you need to charge for your product, in order to cover your costs and make a reasonable profit?

_____
_____

Creating a Questionnaire

INCORPORATING I.T.

Using a computer to type your questionnaire gives it a professional touch. Make sure to bring your prototype with you when carrying out your survey! ☺

(a) Write out two questions you could include in a survey to identify the target market of your product. *(Multiple choice answers are best!)*

- _____
_____
_____

- _____
_____
_____

- _____
_____
_____

(b) Think of two questions for your survey that would identify how much money your target market might spend on your product.

- _____
  _____
  _____

- _____
  _____
  _____

Analysing your Questionnaire

(a) What percentage of those surveyed is interested in purchasing your product?
_____
_____
_____

(b) Who is your target market?
_____
_____
_____

(c) How much are they willing to spend on your product?
_____
_____
_____

(d) Keeping in mind how much it cost to make your product, how much do you think is a reasonable price to charge?
_____
_____
_____

(e) From your research, do you think this is a viable enterprise? Why?
_____
_____
_____

Module 2 – Communication and Enterprise

INCORPORATING I.T.

Using Microsoft Excel or a similar program, create a bar chart displaying some of the findings from your survey. Stick your graph into the box below. ☺

4. Planning

Capital

(a) In order to set up a business, you need a source of income.
List three possible sources of income for your company.

- _____
- _____
- _____

(b) What are the advantages of each type of investment listed above?

- _____
- _____
- _____

(c) What are the disadvantages of each type of investment listed above?

- _____
- _____
- _____

(d) Which source of capital do you think is best for your company? Why?

_____
_____
_____
_____

Setting up a Business Plan

> **Useful TIP!**
> - In order to seek investment from outside, you must create a business plan to show your potential investors how you intend to make a profit. Use the template below to create a business plan for your company. Ask your IT teacher for ideas on how to present your business plan. Remember you want to impress your potential investors! ☺
> - In Chapter 7 you interviewed a representative from a bank or credit union. What information did they suggest you include in a business plan?

1. IDENTITY

Name of business _____

Business address _____

Type of organisation _____

The company logo (Attach your agreed logo design below)

2. BUSINESS DESCRIPTION

What products will you make? Describe in detail.

_____
_____
_____
_____
_____
_____
_____
_____
_____
_____

What are the strengths and weaknesses of your product?

Strengths	**Weaknesses**
_____	_____
_____	_____
_____	_____
_____	_____
_____	_____
_____	_____

3. THE CUSTOMER

Who is the potential customer for your product? Why would they like your product?

_____
_____
_____
_____
_____
_____
_____

4. THE COMPETITION

List other producers of the same product. How do you intend to compete with them?

_____
_____
_____
_____
_____
_____
_____
_____

5. MARKETING

What will be the selling price of your product?

_____

How will the product be distributed to the customer?

_____
_____
_____

What type of packaging will you use?

_____
_____
_____

How will you advertise your product?

_____
_____
_____

6. ORGANISATION AND MANAGEMENT

List the main roles required to operate your enterprise.

- _____
- _____
- _____
- _____
- _____
- _____
- _____
- _____

7. FINANCE

List your sources of finance. Why did you choose these methods?

_____
_____
_____
_____
_____
_____
_____
_____

What is your projected income? (Number of sales x price = projected income.)

_____
_____
_____

What is your projected expenditure (cost of materials, etc.)?

_____
_____
_____

What is your expected profit?

_____
_____
_____

5. Carrying out the Task

Applying for a Job

(a) List the different departments that are required in your company to make it successful. Explain what each department is for.

(i) _____
_____

(ii) _____
_____

(iii) _____

(iv) _____

(v) _____

(b) List all of the jobs that have to be carried out to get your company up and running.

(i) _____

(ii) _____

(iii) _____

(iv) _____

(v) _____

(c) Which of the jobs above would *you* be most interested in? Why?

_____

(d) **Revise Chapter 6: Curriculum Vitae and Letter Writing Skills, Question 12.**
Write the covering letter that you would include with your CV to apply for your preferred job in the mini-company.

_____
_____
_____
_____
/   /20

_____
_____
_____
_____

Dear _____ ,

I refer to your advertisement in _____

_____

_____

_____

_____

_____

_____

_____

_____

_____

Yours _____

_____

Module 2 – Communication and Enterprise

PRACTICAL EXERCISE!

Role play in pairs: one student acts as interviewer and the other as candidate. Present a typed copy of your covering letter and CV in preparation for your interview. Your career guidance teacher could interview you for this job! ☺

INCORPORATING I.T.

A CV is one of the ways in which you impress your prospective employer. Make sure you use Microsoft Word or a similar program to present your work! ☺

(e) Answer the following questions in preparation for your interview:

   (i) How would you describe yourself?

   _____
   _____
   _____
   _____
   _____

   (ii) What do you know about the running of this company?

   _____
   _____
   _____
   _____
   _____

   (iii) What do you know about this particular position?

   _____
   _____
   _____
   _____
   _____
   _____

(iv) Why do you want this position?

(v) What skills do you have that would be particularly useful for this position?

(vi) Do you prefer working as part of a team or working alone? Why?

(vii) What experience do you have in this area?

Meetings

(a) Use the following template to set out an **agenda** for the first meeting of your mini-company. Make sure each of your shareholders receives a copy.

(Insert Company Logo)

AGENDA

Mini-company name _____

Meeting number _____

This meeting will take place at _____

Date _____

Time _____

Programme – General Meeting

Topic	Time allowed
1. _____	_____
2. _____	_____
3. _____	_____
4. _____	_____
5. _____	_____
6. _____	_____
7. _____	_____
8. AOB	_____

Signed: _____
       (General Manager)

Signed: _____
       (Secretary)

Date: _____

Sample agenda

KC

AGENDA

Mini-company name	Kells Cakes
Meeting number	1
This meeting will take place at	Room 26
Date	12 February
Time	1.30 p.m.

Programme – General Meeting

Topic	Time allowed
1. Call to order – General Manager	1.30p.m – 1.31p.m.
2. Attendance check – Personnel Manager	1.31p.m. – 1.35p.m.
3. Production reports – Production Manager	1.35p.m. – 1.40p.m.
4. Projected sales – Sales Manager	1.40p.m. – 1.50p.m.
5. Announcements – General Manager	1.50p.m. – 2.00p.m.
6. AOB	2.00p.m. – 2.10p.m.

Signed: Mark Bradley
(General Manager)

Signed: John Smith
(Secretary)

Date: 12/02/11

(b) Use the following template to take records (Minutes) of all the meetings held by your shareholders. These records should be taken by the Secretary and each shareholder should receive a copy after each meeting.

INCORPORATING I.T.

Minutes and agendas should be typed using Microsoft Word or a similar program. ☺

KC

MINUTES

Monthly meeting of _____ held on _____ at _____ in _____.

Acting chairperson was _____.

Members present:

1. _____	6. _____	11. _____
2. _____	7. _____	12. _____
3. _____	8. _____	13. _____
4. _____	9. _____	14. _____
5. _____	10. _____	15. _____

_____
_____
_____
_____
_____
_____
_____
_____
_____
_____
_____

Approved: Mark Bradley

Signed: John Smith

Sample minutes

MINUTES

Monthly meeting of Kells Cakes held on 12th February at 1.30p.m. in Room 26.

Acting chairperson was Kevin Lynch.

Members present:

1. Mark Bradley
2. John Smith
3. Brian Murphy
4. Orla Farrelly
5. Deirdre Lynch
6. Ursula McMahon
7. Ciaran O'Reilly
8. Mary O'Donoghue
9. James Clarke
10. Dennis O'Loughlin

(a) Production report : Mary O'Donoghue proposed that we make a final decision on the cakes, so that production could begin. Mary suggested that the chocolate cakes would be the most profitable. Ciaran wanted to make vanilla cakes instead. We held a vote and it was decided to select a variety of recipes and to make prototypes of each one to taste and vote on.

(b) Sales report : From the analysis of our questionnaires, Ursula identified our market. She suggested that First Years were our main market and so prices should be geared towards them. She presented her report, showing the expected costs of our ingredients and our projected sales.

(c) AOB : Orla brought it to our attention that Transition Students were to hold a fund-raising day on the 4th, the day before our intended cake sale. She suggested that we change our day of sale to an earlier date so that the fund-raising day would not affect our sales.

(d) Next meeting is to be held on 12 March at 1.30p.m. Room 26 will be unavailable, so a new room will be arranged. Shareholders will be informed of the change in due course.

Approved: Mark Bradley

Signed: John Smith

6. Advertising

(a) **Revise Chapter 9: Advertising** and complete the crossword below.

Across

2. A brief description accompanying a picture (7).
4. A picture or diagram that helps to make something clear or attractive (12).
7. Identifying symbol used by a company (4).
8. Containing a lot of data about the product (11).
10. A brief, catchy phrase used in advertising (6).
11. A class of goods identified by a name (5).

Down

1. What advertisers do to get you to buy the product (5).
3. Real pictures used in advertisements (11).
5. Written material in an advertisement (4).
6. Convincing someone with a good argument (10).
9. The item being advertised (7).

(b) List four ways that you could advertise your product in school.

- _____
- _____
- _____
- _____

(c) Where would be the best place to advertise your product? Give reasons.

_____
_____
_____
_____

(d) What important details would you need to include in your advertisements?

- _____
- _____
- _____
- _____
- _____
- _____

(e) If you were to advertise your product over the school intercom, what would you say? Write the script for your advertisement below:

_____
_____
_____
_____
_____
_____
_____
_____
_____
_____
_____

(f) In the box below, design a poster that you would display in school to advertise your product and mini-company.

[ ]

INCORPORATING I.T.

Use Microsoft Publisher or a similar program to create your advertisement. Make the design modern, eye-catching and original! ☺

7. My Role in the Enterprise

STANDARD ASSIGNMENT

Present a report on your role in the mini-company.

(a) What was your role in the running of this enterprise?

_____

_____

(b) How were you selected for this job?

(c) Describe in detail **your role** in the running of this enterprise.

(d) Describe how you had to consult with other members of the group in order to carry out your role.

(e) Describe a situation where the following managers may have to interact with each other:

- Production Manager and Finance Manager

- Finance Manager and Sales Manager

- Sales Manager and Production Manager

(f) Did you find it difficult working as a member of a team? Explain.

_____

_____

_____

_____

_____

_____

Sample: My Role in the Enterprise

I was Purchasing Manager in this enterprise. To get this job I had to go for an interview. I prepared my CV, wrote a covering letter and sent it to my Career Guidance Teacher. I was called for the interview at 2.00p.m. I wore a neat outfit and made sure that I was on time. I had prepared answers to some questions I thought I might be asked. When I was called into the interview, I sat down and answered all the questions in a clear voice. It was the next day when the Career Guidance Teacher told me I had the job. I was delighted!

As Purchasing Manager, it was my job to buy all the raw materials for this project. We were running a bakery selling a variety of different cakes. We had made a few prototypes and so we had made a final decision on our recipe. I began by making a list of all the ingredients required to make the cakes. I consulted with the Production Manager to make sure I got it right.

When that was done, I had to calculate how much our raw materials would cost. I went to the local Centra and priced the ingredients. They seemed to be too expensive and so we went to Tesco to price the same ingredients to see if we could get them cheaper. Tesco turned out to be a much better option for us and so we decided to buy all the ingredients there. I consulted with the Finance Manager on my research, showing the different prices from both shops and the total cost of our raw materials. The Finance Manager examined my report and gave me the funding for our materials. I bought the ingredients, kept the receipts for the Finance Manager and passed on the raw materials to the Production Manager to take it from there.

I really enjoyed this role because I got to leave school and go to the shops to buy the ingredients. It was a lot of responsibility, being in charge of so much money. It was also a lot of responsibility to get it right. If I bought the wrong ingredients or spent too much, our profits would be affected and the others might get annoyed with me. Luckily everything went to plan.

I also realised how important it is that everyone pulls their own weight. If one person doesn't do their job properly, it really affects the rest of us. I thoroughly enjoyed the experience and would definitely like a job like this in the future!

8. Cross-curricular application

(a) List five subjects that you referred to in order to set up and run your mini-company.

(i) _____

(ii) _____

(iii) _____

(iv) _____

(v) _____

(b) Explain how each of these subjects was used in the running of this company.

(i) _____

(ii) _____

(iii) _____

(iv) _____

(v) _____

Sample Answer For Cross-Curricular Application

I used the following subjects in the running of this company:

- **English and Communications**

  I integrated this subject into the task when I wrote a letter of application for the job and when I wrote and presented my CV. I used Communications when I partook in the mock interview.

- **Hotel, Catering and Tourism**

  I integrated this subject into the task when I used different recipes to make cakes and buns.

- **Vocational Preparation and Guidance**

  I integrated this subject into the task when I set up and ran a successful business.

- **Mathematics**

  I integrated this subject into the task when we calculated the cost of the prototype and when we calculated the profits at the end.

- **I.T.**

  I integrated this subject into the task when I typed and presented my finished Project Folder. I also used IT by using Microsoft Publisher to design logos, advertisements and packaging.

9. Evaluation

(a) What did you enjoy about running the company?

_____

_____

_____

(b) What did you not enjoy?

_____

_____

_____

(c) What skills have you learned as a result of this task?

_____

_____

_____

(d) What did you find you were good at?

_____

_____

_____

(e) What did you find difficult?

_____
_____
_____

(f) From what you learned, would you be interested in running a company in the future?

_____
_____
_____

(g) What advice would you give next year's group when they are setting up their mini-company?

_____
_____
_____

Sample evaluation

> I really enjoyed running this company. It was a lot of work, but I learned a lot. I didn't enjoy having to work as a team. Sometimes other people don't pull their weight and I found I had to do some of their work as well as my own.
>
> My time management skills have improved from working in the mini-company. I was never really good at planning my time, but because we were working to a deadline, I found that I started to improve.
>
> I found that I am good at baking because I was able to follow all of the recipes and the cakes turned out really well.
>
> I found it really difficult to analyse the questionnaires because there were so many of them. This made the research and planning section really difficult.
>
> From what I learned I would really like to run my own business in the future because it's nice to be your own boss and be able to keep any profits made.
>
> If I was to advise next year's group I would tell them to invest their own money rather than selling shares. That way they wouldn't have to share the profits at the end.

Suggestions for your mini-company

It is often difficult to think of ideas for your mini-company. Here is a list of options you might consider.

1. Candle-making.
2. Greeting cards.
3. CD of a local music group.
4. Bakery.
5. Wooden birdhouses.
6. Key-rings.
7. Photo frames.

End of Module Checklist: Communication and Enterprise

At the end of this module, you should have a copy of **each** of the following in your folder to ensure you gain full credits. It is important that you use I.T. wherever possible.

- A typed **REPORT** on an interview with a self-employed person.

- A typed **REPORT** on an interview with a bank or credit union representative.

- A typed **REPORT** on aspects of advertising.

- **Vocational Preparation and Guidance Task** should be presented in a *separate folder*. You must use these headings in your task:

    (a) Brainstorming

    (b) Aims

    (c) Research

    (d) Planning

    (e) Carrying out the Task

    (f) Advertising

    (g) My Role in the Enterprise

    (h) Cross-Curricular Application

    (i) Evaluation

Module THREE

The Communications Media

CHAPTER 10 Newspapers

> ✓ **Useful TIP!**
>
> Bring in samples of both a broadsheet and a tabloid to help you find the answers to the questions in this chapter.

1. Read the clues below and complete the crossword. Use the accompanying images to help you.

Across

2. A newspaper that is sold across a larger area, e.g. across a province (10).
5. Newspapers aimed at commuters or office workers (7).
6. A newspaper sold on week days (5).

Down

1. A newspaper containing stories of interest to people in the immediate area only (5).
3. A newspaper that is available in all parts of the country (8).
4. A newspaper that is sold at weekends only and recaps on the news from the week (6).

2. What is a broadsheet or quality newspaper? Give three examples.

   _____
   _____
   _____

   o _____
   o _____
   o _____

3. What is a tabloid newspaper? Give three examples.

   _____
   _____
   _____

   o _____
   o _____
   o _____

4. Why are local newspapers popular? Give three examples of local newspapers.

   _____
   _____
   _____

   o _____
   o _____
   o _____

5. What is an 'indigenous' newspaper? Give two reasons why we should support our indigenous newspapers.

   _____
   _____
   _____

   o _____
   _____

   o _____
   _____

6. How often do you read newspapers?
   _____
   _____

7. Which type of news stories are most interesting to you? Why?
   _____
   _____

8. Would you be more inclined to read a broadsheet or a tabloid newspaper? Why?
   _____
   _____
   _____

9. Examine the newspaper extract below and comment on each of the terms that follow.

   (a) Banner headline
   _____
   _____
   _____
   _____
   _____
   _____
   _____

   (b) Sub-headings
   _____
   _____
   _____
   _____
   _____
   _____
   _____

(c) Typeface

(d) Caption

(e) Column

10. In relation to a newspaper, what is an editorial? Find an example in your newspaper.

11. What is a feature article? Use your own newspaper to find an example.

12. What does 'circulation' mean in reference to a newspaper?

13. What is meant by the 'readership' of a newspaper?

14. Examine one tabloid and one broadsheet newspaper. Fill in the table below.

Question	Tabloid	Broadsheet
Name the newspaper selected.		
How much does this paper cost?		
What size are the pages?		
How many pages in total are in this newspaper?		
How many stories are covered on the first page?		
Who is the target market for this newspaper?		
Which newspaper uses larger print?		
Which newspaper uses the most colour?		
How many pages relate to sport in each newspaper?		
How many pages relate to business in each newspaper?		
On average, how many photos or graphics are used on each page?		
Where was the paper published?		

Question	Tabloid	Broadsheet
What kinds of stories and reports are dominant in each newspaper?		
Which newspaper has the most text?		
Which newspaper covers the most stories?		
What kinds of products or services are advertised in this paper?		
What is similar about the newspapers?		

15. Explain the following terms.

   (a) Sensationalism

   _____
   _____
   _____

   (b) Objectivity

   _____
   _____
   _____

   (c) Bias

   _____
   _____
   _____

16. Examine the news article below from the *Irish Times* and answer the questions that follow.

Delayed diagnoses could lead to hospital being sued

CAROL COULTER
Legal Affairs Editor

PEOPLE WHO have reduced life expectancy as a result of delayed diagnosis could sue the hospital and doctors involved, according to an expert in medical negligence law, in clear reference to the Tallaght hospital controversy.

In an article in today's Irish Times, barrister John Heal, who has just published a book on medical malpractice, writes that a recent Supreme Court judgement changed the law on compensation for delayed diagnosis.

A case called Philip v Ryan 'greatly liberalised the ability of patients to recover compensation against doctors and hospitals for negligently delayed cancer diagnoses,' he writes.

In this case, a plaintiff recovered €45,000 against the Bon Secours hospital in Cork after diagnosis and treatment of his advanced-stage prostate cancer had been unjustifiably delayed by a period of eight months.

Mr Healy states that the award of compensation was expressly grounded by the Supreme Court in the mental distress and anxiety the plaintiff suffered because of the delay, and additionally his loss of valuable medical opportunities to treat the cancer and the resultant loss to his life expectancy.

He quotes Supreme Court judge Mr Justice Fennelly, who said in the judgment: 'It seems to me to be contrary to instinct and logic that a plaintiff should not be entitled to be compensated for the fact that, due to the negligent diagnosis of his medical condition, he has been deprived of appropriate medical advice and the consequent opportunity to avail of treatment which might improve his condition. I can identify no contrary principle of law or justice…'

(a) In which newspaper would you expect to find this article? Give reasons for your answer.

___

(b) Comment on the headline used in this article. How effective do you think it is?

___

(c) Think of an alternative headline for this article and write it below.

___

(d) On what page of the newspaper would you expect to find this story? Give reasons for your answer.

___

(e) In your own words, explain what this article is about.

_____
_____
_____
_____
_____
_____
_____
_____
_____

(f) Comment on the language used in this article. Did you find it easy or difficult to understand?

_____
_____
_____

(g) Who, do you think, is the target audience for this article? Give reasons for your answer.

_____
_____
_____
_____
_____
_____
_____

(h) Would you say this article is biased or objective? Give reasons for your answer.

_____
_____
_____

(i) What graphics or photographs do you think might be suitable to accompany this article?

_____
_____
_____

17. Examine the news article below from the *Irish Times* and answer the questions that follow.

DISGRACEFUL & UNACCEPTABLE

HSE chief blasts X-ray scandal

By **Gary Meneely**

HSE boss Brendan Drumm broke his silence on the X-ray scandal yesterday admitting it was 'a disgrace and totally unacceptable'.

A whistleblower revealed last Tuesday how 58,000 adult X-rays taken over five years at Tallaght Hospital were never reviewed by a consultant radiologist.

The following day the controversy deepened after it emerged 30,000 GP referral letters lay unopened at the Dublin hospital.

But despite confidence in the health service hitting a new low, it has taken Prof Drumm almost a week to speak up.

During a radio interview he said: 'It was totally unacceptable and appalling that letters were unanswered and that should have serious consequences.'

But Drumm refused to take responsibility for the debacle – like Health Minister Mary Harney who has remained on a jaunt to New Zealand.

Two cancer patients received a delayed diagnosis as a result of their X-rays not being read by experts.

One has since died while the other is being treated at the hospital.

Opposition politicians have blasted the HSE boss. Fine Gael health spokesman Dr James Reilly stormed: 'Professor Drumm's first interview after nearly a week of silence is a bitter blow to patients. His handwashing and refusal to accept responsibility was reminiscent of Pontius Pilate.

'It beggars belief that the head of the organisations which supplies 200 million to Tallaght Hospital seems to have no hand, act or part in ensuring that the hospital is run in a safe fashion....'

(a) In which newspaper would you expect to find this article? Give reasons for your answer.

_____
_____
_____

(b) Comment on the headline used in this article. How effective do you think it is?

_____
_____
_____

(c) Think of an alternative headline for this article and write it below.

_____
_____

(d) On what page of the newspaper would you expect to find this story? Give reasons for your answer.

_____
_____
_____

(e) In your own words, explain what this article is about.

_____
_____
_____
_____

(f) Comment on the language used in this article. Was there any slang or sensational language used? Give examples.

_____
_____
_____
_____

(g) Who is the target audience for this article? Give reasons for your answer.

_____
_____
_____
_____

(h) Would you say this article is biased or objective? Give reasons for your answer.

_____
_____
_____

(i) What graphics or photographs do you think might be suitable to include with this article?

_____
_____
_____
_____

STANDARD ASSIGNMENT

Study coverage of a particular event or news story in <u>two</u> newspapers and write a short report on the differences and similarities between the newspapers.

Writing your Report

Follow the instructions below to write up your report.

1. Select two newspapers: one broadsheet and one tabloid.

2. Select an article in the broadsheet and find a corresponding story on the same event in the tabloid.

3. Compare and contrast the stories under the following headings:
   - Headline
   - Language and sensationalism
   - Graphics
   - Target audience
   - Position in the newspaper
   - Length of the text
   - Objectivity and bias

4. Decide which newspaper handled the story better, in your opinion.

5. **Revise Chapter 4: Writing a Report**, then complete the report template below.

Title: _____

Purpose: _____

_____

_____

_____

Findings: _____

_____

_____

_____

_____

_____

_____

_____

Conclusions: _____

🅮 INCORPORATING I.T.

Type your report using Microsoft Word or a similar program.
Why not use some illustrations and pictures in your report?
You could also use PowerPoint to help you present your report to your class! ☺

📝 ADVANCED ASSIGNMENT

Write your own account of an event or news item. Prepare it for inclusion in a newspaper and give it an appropriate heading.

Write a newspaper article using all the information you have gained from this chapter. Your article can be a report on something local, e.g. a recent school event or local football game.

Revise Chapter 4: Writing a Report, then follow the instructions below to write your article.

1. Select the topic for your article.
2. Decide whether your article would appear in a tabloid or a broadsheet.
3. Give your article an appropriate heading.
4. Examine your main findings.

5. What conclusions can you draw after carrying out your investigation?

6. Fill out the template below.

Title: _____

Purpose: _____
_____
_____
_____
_____

Findings: _____
_____
_____
_____
_____
_____
_____
_____
_____
_____

Conclusions: _____
_____
_____
_____
_____
_____
_____
_____

INCORPORATING I.T.

Use a computer to type your report. Choose the appropriate fonts and typefaces throughout. 😊

PRACTICAL EXERCISE!

- Why not create a school newspaper? Each student writes an article to be included in the newspaper. You can assemble and print it using Microsoft Publisher or a similar program! 😊

- You have also learned at this stage how to write a review. Why not write reviews for your school newspaper? You could review films, local football games or even CDs! 😊

CHAPTER 11 Radio

1. Why is radio still popular today, even with the invention of the television?

   _____

   _____

   _____

   _____

2. Name one national and one local radio station:

   National _____

   Local _____

3. What are the advantages of local radio over national radio?

   _____

   _____

   _____

   _____

   _____

4. What type of programme is each of the following:

   (a) Current Affairs

   _____

   (b) Weather

   _____

   (c) Sport

   _____

   (d) Talkback radio

   _____

   (e) Music

   _____

(f) Religious affairs

5. Describe what is involved when sending a request to a radio station.

6. Describe what would be involved in entering a radio competition.

7. What is the main appeal of phone-in programmes for listeners?

8. What are the advantages of phone-in programmes for a radio station?

9. What is your favourite radio station? Why?

10. What is your favourite programme? Why?

Beat! LCA English Assignments Workbook

11. The following is an extract from the radio listings taken from *The Irish Times*. It lists schedules for RTÉ Radio 1 and RTÉ 2FM.

RTÉ Radio 1

FM: 88.2–90.0; 95.2mHz; LW: 252kHz.

News on the Hour. **5.30a.m.** *Risin' Time.* **7.00a.m.** *Morning Ireland* **9.00a.m.** *The John Murray Show.* **10.00a.m.** *Today with Pat Kenny.* Followed by *The Angelus.* **12.00** *The Ronan Collins Show.* **1.00p.m.** *News.* **1.45p.m.** *Liveline.* Conversation with phone-in. **3.00p.m.** *Mooney.* **4.30p.m.** *Drivetime.* **7.00p.m.** *Sport at 7.* **7.30p.m.** *Arena.* A look at the latest news from the world of arts and entertainment, presented by Sean Rocks. **8.30p.m.** *The John Creedon Show.* A blend of contemporary, Irish and international music. **9.50p.m.** *Nuacht.* **10.00p.m.** *Arts Tonight.* Presented by Vincent Woods. **11.00p.m.** *News; Sport News.* **11.15p.m.** *Book on One*: *Cailíní Beaga Ghleann na mBláth*, by Éilis Ní Dhuibhne. Read by Doireann Ní Bhriain. **11.25p.m.** *Late Date.* **2.00a.m.** *Through the Night*: *The Tubridy Show.* **2.30a.m.** *Today with Pat Kenny.* **3.30a.m.** *Liveline* **4.00a.m.** *Miriam Meets…* **5.00a.m.** *Bowman: Sunday*

RTÉ 2FM

FM: 90.4–92.2; 97.0 mHz.

6.00a.m. *The Colm and Jim-Jim Breakfast Show.* **9.00a.m.** *The Tubridy Show.* **12.00** *Rick O'Shea.* **3.00p.m.** *Larry Gogan's Golden Hour.* **4.00p.m.** *The Will Leahy Show.* **7.00p.m.** *Dave Fanning.* **9.00p.m.** *Dan Hegarty.* **11.00p.m.** *Damien Farrelly.* **1.00a.m.** *2FM Replay.*

(a) Look at the listings for RTÉ Radio 1. Give an example of each type of programme listed below and its time slot.

   (i)   Current affairs _____ Time _____

   (ii) Sport _____ Time _____

   (iii) Drama _____ Time _____

   (iv) Talkback _____ Time _____

   (v) Religion _____ Time _____

(b) What type of programming is offered by RTÉ 2FM?

_____

_____

_____

_____

_____

(c) What programme is on RTÉ Radio 1 at 9.00 a.m.? Why do you think it is on at this time? Who is it aimed at?

(d) What programme is on RTÉ Radio 1 at 11.15p.m.? Why do you think this time is suitable for this programme?

(e) In general, who do you think is the target audience for RTÉ Radio 1? Refer to the list of programmes in your answer.

(f) Looking at the list of programmes on RTÉ 2FM, who do you think is the target audience? Explain your answer.

(g) Of the two radio stations above, which would you prefer to listen to? Explain your answer.

Beat! LCA English Assignments Workbook

Listening to Radio Programmes

Part 1

CD - Track 6

1. Track 6 on the accompanying CD is an extract from Dave Fanning's radio show on RTÉ 2FM. Listen to the extract (more than once, if necessary) and answer the following questions.

    (a) What kind of radio show is this?

    _____
    _____

    (b) Who do you think is the target audience for this programme? Explain your answer.

    _____
    _____
    _____
    _____

    (c) What time slot do you think would be appropriate for this programme? Explain your answer.

    _____
    _____
    _____
    _____

    (d) Who is being interviewed in this programme?

    _____
    _____

    (e) What is being discussed?

    _____
    _____
    _____

    (f) Would you be interested in listening to this programme? Why? Why not?

    _____
    _____
    _____

Part 2

CD - Track 7

2. Track 7 on the accompanying CD is an extract from *Liveline* with Joe Duffy on RTÉ Radio 1. Listen to the extract (more than once, if necessary) and answer the following questions.

(a) What kind of radio show is this?

_____

_____

(b) Who do you think is the target audience for this programme? Explain your answer.

_____

_____

_____

_____

(c) What time slot do you think would be appropriate for this programme? Explain your answer.

_____

_____

_____

_____

(d) Who is being interviewed in this programme?

_____

_____

(e) What is being discussed?

_____

_____

_____

(f) Would you be interested in ringing in to this programme? Why? Why not?

_____

_____

_____

3. After listening to both extracts, which programme would you be most likely to listen to again? Why?

Visiting your Local Station

STANDARD ASSIGNMENT

Visit your local radio station and present a report on your visit. If you cannot visit a radio station, visit your local newspaper office and tailor the questions accordingly.

1. Name the radio station.

2. Is this a local or national radio station?

3. How big is the audience for this station?

4. What kinds of programmes are played on this radio station?

5. What factors must be kept in mind when choosing a time slot for each programme?

6. Radio stations can be large employers. What jobs are available at a radio station?

7. What qualifications do you need to work in a radio station?

8. What is the target audience of the radio station? Does it vary?

9. Radio stations play a lot of music. Who supplies the CDs?

10. How does the radio station make money?

11. For talkback radio programmes, is there much research to be done? Why? Why not?

12. What kind of equipment is required for a radio station?

13. Write **three** other questions you would like answered from your visit to the radio station.

   (a)

   (b)

Beat! LCA English Assignments Workbook

(c) _____

> ✓ **Useful TIP!**
>
> **Revise Chapter 4: Writing a Report**, then use the template below to write your own report.

Title: _____

Purpose: _____

_____

_____

_____

_____

Findings: _____

_____

_____

_____

_____

_____

_____

_____

_____

Conclusions: _____

_____

_____

_____

_____

_____

_____

INCORPORATING I.T.

Type your report using Microsoft Word or a similar program. Remember to save a record of your work and hand a hard copy to your teacher! ☺

Conducting a Radio Survey

ADVANCED ASSIGNMENT

Conduct a survey on radio listening and present your findings in a report.

LESSON BOX!

Organising a Questionnaire

It is not easy to create a good questionnaire. Begin by deciding who the questionnaire is aimed at, e.g. teenagers, adults, business people, unemployed people, etc. You must also be clear about what information you are seeking. Then decide the scale of your survey, i.e. how many questionnaires you are going to analyse.

Once this is done, you can focus on the questions. Most questions should be kept simple, with 'yes' or 'no' answers. Sometimes multiple choice questions works well, e.g. 'Do you buy the paper: (a) everyday, (b) once a week, (c) less often?' Limit the number of questions requiring a statement as an answer, as they are more difficult to analyse.

Preparation for your survey

1. Who is this survey aimed at?

   _____

   _____

   _____

2. What information are you hoping to find by doing this survey?

   _____

   _____

   _____

3. What is the scale of your survey? (How many people are you going to survey?)

   _____
   _____

4. Write at least **five** questions that you intend to include in your questionnaire:

   Question 1 _____
   _____

   Question 2 _____
   _____

   Question 3 _____
   _____

   Question 4 _____
   _____

   Question 5 _____
   _____

5. Type your questionnaire using Microsoft Word or a similar program. Print or photocopy multiples of your questionnaire, making sure to save your original. Hand out the questionnaire to be completed by your target group.

6. Complete the following report:

   Title: _____

   Purpose: _____
   _____
   _____
   _____
   _____

   Findings: _____
   _____
   _____
   _____
   _____
   _____
   _____

Conclusions: _____

🌐 INCORPORATING I.T.

Why not present your findings using graphs? Make out a table of your results using Microsoft Excel or a similar program. Presenting your results in graph form will make them very easy to interpret! ☺

⚙ PRACTICAL EXERCISE!

Create your own radio programme in class! Work on the preparation or recording of a short radio programme to be aired on your public address system in school. Use the following pointers:

- Name your radio station.
- Create a jingle for your programme.
- Be clear about your target audience.
- Decide on the content of your programme.
- Pick suitable music to be used.
- Think of any sound effects you might need.
- Decide how long your programme should be.
- Choose a time for airing the programme.
- Write a report on the entire experience.

CHAPTER 12 Television

1. Do you think people watch too much television? Explain your answer.

   _____

   _____

2. Do you think that television is merely entertaining or is it also educational? Explain your answer.

   _____

   _____

   _____

3. Look at the television schedule for TV3 below and answer the questions that follow.

   > **6.10a.m.** Tonight with Vincent Browne. **7.00a.m.** Ireland AM. **10.00a.m.** The Jeremy Kyle Show. **11.00a.m.** The Morning Show with Sybil and Martin. **11.50a.m.** Midday. **1.20p.m.** The Oprah Winfrey Show. **2.10p.m.** The Ellen Degeneres Show. **3.05p.m.** Emmerdale. **3.30p.m.** Coronation Street. **4.00p.m.** Coronation Street. **4.30p.m.** Judge Judy. **5.30p.m.** News at 5.30. Followed by Weather and 3 Update. **6.00p.m.** Xposé. A daily look at Hollywood and beyond. **6.30p.m.** Friends. Ross confides a sexual fantasy to Rachel, who can't keep a secret. Meanwhile, Chandler resumes an old relationship. **7.00p.m.** The Krypton Factor. Contestants battle for the last of the semi-final places. Four tests – mental agility, observation, general knowledge and the assault course – will decide the winner. **8.00p.m.** Beware: Thieves on the Street II. Documentary which uses CCTV footage and frank interviews with thieves to expose the tricks used by pickpockets and show how potential victims are targeted. **9.00p.m.** Three Kings (1999). Satirical action drama set after the Gulf War, in which four soldiers go AWOL and head for secret Iraqi bunkers marked on a map where they believe looted Kuwaiti gold is being held. With George Clooney and Mark Wahlberg. **11.05p.m.** Nightly News. **11.10p.m.** Tonight with Vincent Browne. **12.00** Cult Killer: The Ricky Rodriguez Story. Documentary uncovering the chilling case of Ricky Rodriguez, who stabbed his former nanny to death and then shot himself, seemingly from trauma from childhood sexual abuse. **1.00a.m.** The Graham Norton Show. **1.55a.m.** Eleventh Hour. **2.45a.m.** Close.

   © Irish Daily Star Chic

(a) Fill in the table below, giving examples of each type of programme, its time slot and its target audience.

Programme type	Example	Time slot	Target audience
Sitcom			
News			
Talk show			
Celebrity			
Soap opera			
Game show			
Current affairs			
Film			
Documentary			

(b) At 12.00 midnight, a documentary is being shown. Why do you think this documentary is on so late? Why is it not scheduled for day-time television?

_____
_____
_____

(c) *The Oprah Winfrey Show* is scheduled for 1.20p.m. Why do you think this show is scheduled so early in the day? Who is it aimed at?

_____
_____
_____

(d) The film *Three Kings* is scheduled for 9.00p.m. Why do you think this is a suitable time for this film?

_____
_____
_____

(e) What is meant by the term 'watershed'? Looking at this TV schedule, what time do you think the watershed happens?

_____
_____
_____

(f) Explain **three** reasons why time slots are so important when placing a programme in the schedule.

- _____
- _____
- _____

Creating your own TV Station Schedule

1. Imagine you have your own television station. You must choose a selection of programmes that will appeal to a range of different audiences.

   (a) What are your favourite programmes on TV?

   _____
   _____

(b) What time do you think these programmes should be on television? Why?

(c) What programme do you think would appeal most to children under the age of ten?

(d) What time do you think these programmes should be shown? Why?

(e) What types of programme do you think would appeal mostly to women? Why?

(f) What time do you think these programmes should be scheduled? Why?

(g) What programmes do you think would appeal mostly to men? Why?

(h) What would be an appropriate time slot for these programmes? Why?

(i) What programmes would appeal mostly to teenagers and young adults?

(j) What time slot would suit these programmes? Give reasons for your answer.

(k) Select a suitable documentary for your station. Who is the target audience?

(l) What time slot is appropriate for your documentary?

_____

_____

2. Looking back at the answers you wrote for Question 1 above, revise the TV3 schedule on page 132, adapting it for your own TV station. Fill in the timetable below and remember to keep your audience in mind when selecting suitable time slots.

Time	Programme

STANDARD ASSIGNMENT

OPTION 1: Plan a TV schedule for one evening, taking into account time slots, target audience and variety of programming. Present a report on your findings.

3. Write a report explaining why you selected each of the programmes in your TV schedule. Describe your target audience and explain why you chose particular time slots. Use the template below for your report.

Title: _____

Purpose: _____
_____
_____
_____
_____
_____

Reasons for choosing each programme: _____
_____
_____
_____
_____

Reasons for particular time slots: _____
_____
_____
_____
_____

Conclusions (explaining what was difficult or easy): _____
_____
_____
_____
_____

INCORPORATING I.T.

Type your finished report using Microsoft Word or a similar program. Remember to keep a saved copy for yourself and give a hard copy to your teacher. ☺

Soap Operas

1. What is a soap opera? Give **three** examples and list what channels show them.
   _____
   _____
   _____

2. Of the three soap operas you named, list **five** things they have in common.

   (a) _____
   _____

   (b) _____
   _____

   (c) _____
   _____

   (d) _____
   _____

   (e) _____
   _____

3. In your opinion, what makes soap operas so popular?
   _____
   _____
   _____

4. What kinds of social issues are portrayed in soap operas? Give examples.
   _____
   _____
   _____
   _____

5. Do you think soap operas reflect real life or do you think they are exaggerated? Explain your answer.
   _____
   _____
   _____
   _____

6. What time are soap operas normally aired? Why do you think this is so?

_____

_____

_____

Examining a soap opera of your choice

1. Select one soap opera. Who is the target audience of this programme? Explain your answer.

_____

_____

_____

2. How often is this soap opera aired?

_____

_____

3. Where is the soap opera set?

_____

_____

4. Select one of the main characters in this soap opera and answer the questions below.

    (a) Name the character.

    _____

    (b) Describe a storyline involving this character.

    _____

    _____

    _____

    _____

    (c) How does this character dress? Why do you think these outfits were chosen?

    _____

    _____

    _____

    _____

(d) Do you think that this character is stereotypical? Explain your answer.

_____
_____
_____

(e) Describe the lifestyle and general values of this character.

_____
_____
_____

(f) Comment on the language used by this character.

_____
_____
_____

5. How many storylines run in a soap opera at any one time? Why do writers include more than one storyline?

_____
_____
_____

6. Are the storylines in soap operas serious or humorous? Why? Explain your answer.

_____
_____
_____
_____

7. What is meant by a cliffhanger ending? What is the purpose of a cliffhanger?

_____
_____
_____
_____

8. Do you watch soap operas? Why? Why not?

_____
_____
_____

Review of a TV programme

STANDARD ASSIGNMENT

OPTION 2: Complete a review of a TV programme, film or documentary.

Record a TV drama, a televised version of a novel or a documentary on the life of a literary figure. Watch the programme in class and answer the questions that follow. This will be the basis for writing your review.

1. What is being reviewed?

2. To what genre does it belong?

3. Who are the main characters?

4. What time is it shown on TV?

5. Describe the setting.

6. What is the plot?

7. Does the programme or film achieve what it set out to do? Why? Why not?

8. Comment on the script or dialogue.

_____
_____
_____

9. Give your own opinion of the programme or film. Who do you think might be interested in watching it?

_____
_____
_____

10. **Revise Chapter 5: Writing a Review.** Using your answers to the questions above, write out your review of this programme or film.

_____
_____
_____
_____
_____
_____
_____
_____
_____
_____
_____
_____
_____
_____

INCORPORATING I.T.

- Type your finished review using Microsoft Word or a similar program. Save your review and give a hard copy to your teacher. You could include this review in your school magazine. ☺

Module 3 – The Communications Media

11. Most TV Series' can be purchased as a Box Set. Imagine you are buying a Box Set as a gift for a friend. Name the TV Series.

_____

_____

12. Explain why you think this would be a good gift.

_____

_____

_____

_____

13. Write out the blurb that you would expect to find on the back of the cover of the Box Set. What information would it include?

_____

_____

_____

_____

_____

_____

_____

_____

PRACTICAL EXERCISE!

Examine the Box Set Cover below. Design a cover for the TV Box Set selected in Question 11. Include images and a written blurb.

INCORPORATING I.T.

- Using Microsoft Publisher re-create your design in a professional way. Do you think customers would like your design? Why? Why not? ☺

143

CHAPTER 13 Aspects of Film

1. Read the following film reviews and answer the questions.

HEAT'S TOP TEN DVDS
THE BEST DVDS FOR YOU TO BUY OR RENT RIGHT NOW!

1 GLEE: SEASON ONE, VOLUME TWO – ROAD TO REGIONALS (12)
Matthew Morrison, Jane Lynch
Relive the second half of the hit series here or with the complete Season One DVD. SEE REVIEW ★★★★★

2 KICK-ASS (15)
Aaron Johnson, Nicolas Cage
Stardust director Matthew Vaughn provocatively reinvents the superhero flick, with geeky teens and profane 11-year-old killing machine Hit-Girl. ★★★★★

3 FOUR LIONS (15)
Riz Ahmed, Kayvan Novak
Chris (*Brass Eye*) Morris' typically maverick and frequently great comedy milks laughs from slapstick suicide bombers. A word-of-mouth cinema hit. ★★★★

4 PRINCE OF PERSIA: THE SANDS OF TIME (12)
Jake Gyllenhaal, Gemma Arterton
A lack of star chemistry takes the fizz out of an otherwise handsomely staged action spectacular. SEE REVIEW ★★★

5 LOST: THE FINAL SEASON (15)
Matthew Fox, Evangeline Lilly
At last, all the answers you've been waiting for! (Except the really important ones.) Find out what the fuss was about with the final, supernatural season. SEE REVIEWS EXTRA ★★★

6 DEAR JOHN (12)
Channing Tatum, Amanda Seyfried
Adapted from a novel by *The Notebook*'s Nicholas Sparks, this love-against-the-odds romantic drama is more of the same. No complaints from us, then. ★★★

7 THE LAST SONG (PG)
Miley Cyrus, Liam Hemsworth
Yet another movie adapted from a book by Nicholas Sparks (see *Dear John*, above). Here, young love blossoms at the beach. ★★★

8 DATE NIGHT (15)
Steve Carell, Tina Fey
James Franco and Mark Wahlberg bag the winning roles in this comedy-cum-action flick. Thumbs up for the laughs, but we're not so sure about the action. ★★★

9 BIG BROTHER'S BIG DVD (15)
Loads of *Big Brother* housemates
A big commemorative collection of episodes from the last 11 years of Channel 4's groundbreaking Reality TV show. There's also a heap of best bits for your viewing pleasure. ★★★★★

10 MISTRESSES: SERIES THREE (15)
Sarah Parish, Shelley Conn
The last four-episode hurrah of one of our favourite homegrown TV dramas of recent years. Goodbye, *Mistresses*, we will miss you terribly. ★★★★★

(a) Name the genre of each of these films.
  - *Date Night*
  - *Kick-Ass*
  - *Dear John*
  - *The Last Song*
  - *Four Lions*
  - *Prince of Persia*

(b) Name two films from the list that are aimed at men.

(c) Name two films from the list that are aimed at women.

(d) Which genre is your favourite? Why?

(e) Which film from the list would you be most likely to watch? Explain your answer.

144

2. What is the role of each of the following in the making of a film?

   (a) Screenwriter

   _____
   _____
   _____

   (b) Director

   _____
   _____
   _____

   (c) Producer

   _____
   _____
   _____

   (d) Camera crew

   _____
   _____
   _____

   (e) Editor

   _____
   _____
   _____

3. Technical terms:

   Look at the photos below and choose the correct label for each one.

   - Close-up shot.
   - Medium shot.
   - Long shot.

   (i) _____   (ii) _____   (iii) _____

Film Glossary

Across

1. A series of shots put together to create the action of one section of time (5).
2. Joining the film together using all the different shots taken (4).
4. Action that has taken place in an earlier time but is now being recalled on screen (9).
9. The height of the camera in relation to the subject (6,5).
11. The person in charge of the whole film (8).

Down

1. The written script, action and stage directions (10).
3. When the camera moves across the whole scene (3).
5. The music used in the film (10).
6. The conversations that the characters have on screen (8).
7. The category of film (5).
8. A shot showing only some of the features of the subject (5,2).
10. This is when the camera moves forward (or backwards) following the action (8).
12. One shot finishes and another shot appears on screen straight away (3).

4. Select a film to watch in class. First, watch it in full and then watch it a second time scene by scene. Answer the following questions.

Mise en scène

(a) Describe the plot of the film.

___
___
___

(b) To what genre does this film belong?

___
___

(c) Describe the setting. Is it important in the film? Comment on background, props, colour, lighting, etc.

___
___
___

(d) Who are the main characters? What are their roles in the film? Comment on action, gesture, facial expressions, costumes, etc.

___
___
___
___
___

(e) What sort of conflict occurs during the development of the plot?

___
___
___

Sound and effects

(f) Comment on the dialogue in the film (i.e. language and script).

___
___
___

(g) What kind of music was used throughout the film? Comment on the tempo, genre and era of the music.

_____
_____
_____

(h) What kinds of special effects are used in this film? Do you think they are effective?

_____
_____
_____

Editing

(i) Comment on how separate shots are linked together to tell the story.

_____
_____

Camera shots

(j) Find a specific example of each of the following camera shots in your chosen film. Explain how each shot works to make a scene more effective.

- Medium shot _____
_____

- High-angle shot _____
_____

- Sharp focus _____
_____

- Zoom shot _____
_____

- Tracking _____
_____

- Pan shot _____
_____

STANDARD ASSIGNMENT

Complete a short study of aspects of film and present a report on your findings.

5. Using your answers to Question 4, write a report on aspects of film. Use the template below and type your report using Microsoft Word or a similar program.

Title: _____

Purpose: _____

_____

_____

_____

Findings: _____

_____

_____

_____

_____

_____

_____

_____

_____

_____

Conclusions: _____

_____

_____

_____

_____

_____

Sample Film Report

Title

Into the West, directed by Mike Newell.

Purpose

We selected *Into the West* for this report as it is a well-known Irish film. It is about two young Traveller brothers seeking a life of adventure. Their mother dies in childbirth, leaving her husband to raise the boys alone in a poor north Dublin housing estate. Their grandfather fills their imagination with traditional Irish stories and when a white horse appears to follow him home from the sea one day, it begins a whole new adventure for the two young boys. The purpose of this report is to identify the different techniques used by the director in making this film. We decided to focus our report on the opening sequence.

In the opening scene we get a real sense of mystery as the white horse gallops across the shore at night. The director creates this mystery by contrasting the white horse against the darkness. There is music in the background only – a song called 'The Blue Sea and the White Horse'. This is a *leitmotif*, a piece of music or signature tune that is associated with the horse throughout the film. The music helps to create the scene, bringing to mind traditional Ireland.

We then see an old man. It is clear by his scruffy appearance and ragged clothes that he is poor, possibly a Traveller. When he arrives at the campsite in his caravan, this is confirmed. A close-up camera shot shows us the old man's face as he sees the horse for the first time. Clearly, he cannot believe what he is seeing.

Conclusion

Judging by the opening sequence, we can see how Newell created a mystical atmosphere. The music, costume and props were selected carefully by the director to tell the story. It is obvious that Newell has done an effective job, as we have yet to hear any dialogue but the story still unfolds before our eyes. For these reasons, I admire Newell as a director.

ADVANCED ASSIGNMENT

Create a storyboard for a new film!

6. Imagine you are creating the storyboard for a new film. Before you begin, complete these questions.

   (a) What genre of film would you like to create?

   (b) Where will the story take place?

   (c) Who are the characters involved in the action?

   (d) Describe the setting of your film. Give details about time and place.

   (e) Briefly outline the plot of the film. What conflict will occur and how will it be resolved?

   (f) Write the dialogue and stage directions for the scene.

PRACTICAL EXERCISE!

Now that you have worked on a storyboard, why not try filming a scene? Using your script and your chosen setting, record your scene on a camcorder. Download Windows Movie Maker from the Internet so that you can create and edit scenes. You can also delete bad scenes and piece together your finished film with just a few clicks! Ask your I.T. teacher for help. Good luck! ☺

End of Module Checklist: The Communications Media

At the end of this module you should have a copy of **each** of the following in your folder to ensure you gain full credits. It is important that you use I.T. wherever possible.

- A typed **REPORT** on the similarities and differences between coverage of a particular news event in a tabloid and in a broadsheet.
- A typed **NEWS ARTICLE**, with an appropriate headline, for inclusion in a newspaper.
- A typed **REPORT** on your visit to a radio station or newspaper office.
- A typed **QUESTIONNAIRE** on radio listenership patterns and a written presentation of your findings from the survey.
- A typed **REPORT** on TV scheduling, including an explanation of your own programming choices and selected time slots.
- A typed **REVIEW** of a film, TV programme or documentary.
- A typed **REPORT** on aspects of film.
- A **STORYBOARD** for a new film.

Module FOUR

Critical Literacy and Composition

CHAPTER 14 The Poetry of Popular Song

1. The following is Chris de Burgh's song, *The Spanish Train*. Read the lyrics and if possible listen to a recording of the song. Then answer the questions that follow.

Spanish Train

There's a Spanish train that runs between Guadalquivir and old Seville.
And at dead of night the whistle blows
and people hear she's running still...

And then they hush their children back to sleep,
lock the doors, upstairs they creep,
for it is said that the souls of the dead
fill that train ten thousand deep!

Well, a railwayman lay dying with his people by his side.
His family were crying, knelt in prayer before he died,
but above his bed just a-waiting for the dead
was the Devil with a twinkle in his eye.
'Well, God's not around and look what I've found: this one's mine!'

Just then the Lord himself appeared in a blinding flash of light
and shouted at the devil, 'Get thee hence to endless night!'
But the Devil just grinned and said, 'I may have sinned,
but there's no need to push me around.
I got him first so you can do your worst –
he's going underground!'

'But I think I'll give you one more chance,' said the Devil with a smile.
'So throw away that stupid lance – it's really not your style.
Joker is the name, poker is the game.
We'll play right here on this bed
and then we'll bet for the biggest stakes yet:
the souls of the dead!'

And I said, 'Look out, Lord, he's going to win.
The sun is down and the night is riding in.
That train is dead on time, many souls are on the line.
Oh Lord, he's going to win!'

Well, the railwayman he cut the cards
and he dealt them each a hand of five.
And for the Lord he was praying hard
or that train he'd have to drive...
Well the Devil he had three aces and a king
and the Lord, he was running for a straight.
He had the queen and the knave and the nine and ten of spades –
all he needed was the eight...

154

And then the Lord he called for one more card,
but he drew the diamond eight.
And the Devil said to the son of God,
'I believe you've got it straight.
So deal me one for the time has come
to see who'll be the king of this place.'
But as he spoke, from beneath his cloak
he slipped another ace...

<u>Ten thousand souls was the opening bid
and it soon went up to fifty nine,
but the Lord didn't see what the Devil did
and he said: 'That suits me fine.
I'll raise you high to hundred and five
and forever put an end to your sins.'
But the Devil let out a mighty shout: 'My hand wins!'</u>

*And I said, 'Look out, Lord, he's going to win.
The sun is down and the night is riding in.
That train is dead on time, many souls are on the line.
Oh Lord, he's going to win!'*

Well that Spanish train still runs between
Guadalquivir and old Seville.
And at dead of night the whistle blows
and people fear she's running still...
And far away in some recess
The Lord and the Devil are now playing chess.
The Devil still cheats and wins more souls
and, as for the Lord, well, he's just doing his best...

*And I said, 'Look out, Lord, he's going to win.
The sun is down and the night is riding in.
That train is dead on time, many souls are on the line.
Oh Lord, he's going to win!'*

(a) Where does the action in this song take place?

_____
_____
_____

(b) What characters are involved?

_____
_____
_____

(c) Describe what happens in the song.

_____
_____
_____
_____
_____

(d) What do you think is the main theme of the song? Explain your answer.

_____
_____
_____
_____

(e) What is the atmosphere of the song? Refer in your answer to both the lyrics and the music.

(f) Looking at the lyrics only, what are the indications that they could be suitably set to music? Refer to rhyme, rhythm and repetition in your answer.

(g) Explain what is happening in the underlined section of the song.

(h) What is your opinion of the above song? Comment on both the lyrics and the music.

2. Read the lyrics below and listen to a performance of this song by Johnny Cash if possible. Then answer the questions that follow.

A Boy Named Sue

My daddy left home when I was three
And he didn't leave much to ma and me
Just this old guitar and an empty bottle of booze.
Now, I don't blame him cause he run and hid
But the meanest thing that he ever did
Was before he left, he went and named me "Sue."

Well, he must o' thought that is quite a joke
And it got a lot of laughs from a' lots of folk,
It seems I had to fight my whole life through.
Some gal would giggle and I'd get red
And some guy'd laugh and I'd bust his head,
I tell ya, life ain't easy for a boy named "Sue."

Well, I grew up quick and I grew up mean,
My fist got hard and my wits got keen,
I'd roam from town to town to hide my shame.
But I made a vow to the moon and stars
That I'd search the honky-tonks and bars
And kill that man who gave me that awful name.

Well, it was Gatlinburg in mid-July
And I just hit town and my throat was dry,
I thought I'd stop and have myself a brew.
At an old saloon on a street of mud,
There at a table, dealing stud,
Sat the dirty, mangy dog that named me "Sue."

Well, I knew that snake was my own sweet dad
From a worn-out picture that my mother'd had,
And I knew that scar on his cheek and his evil eye.
He was big and bent and gray and old,
And I looked at him and my blood ran cold
And I said: "My name is 'Sue!' How do you do!
Now you're gonna die!!"

Well, I hit him hard right between the eyes
And he went down, but to my surprise,
He come up with a knife and cut off a piece of my ear.

But I busted a chair right across his teeth
And we crashed through the wall and into the street
Kicking and a' gouging in the mud and the blood and the beer.

I tell ya, I've fought tougher men
But I really can't remember when,
He kicked like a mule and he bit like a crocodile.
I heard him laugh and then I heard him cuss,
He went for his gun and I pulled mine first,
He stood there lookin' at me and I saw him smile.

And he said: "Son, this world is rough
And if a man's gonna make it, he's gotta be tough
And I knew I wouldn't be there to help ya along.
So I give ya that name and I said goodbye
I knew you'd have to get tough or die
And it's the name that helped to make you strong."

He said: "Now you just fought one hell of a fight
And I know you hate me, and you got the right
To kill me now, and I wouldn't blame you if you do.
But ya ought to thank me, before I die,
For the gravel in ya guts and the spit in ya eye
Cause I'm the son-of-a-bitch that named you "Sue."'

I got all choked up and I threw down my gun
And I called him my pa, and he called me his son,
And I came away with a different point of view.
And I think about him, now and then,
Every time I try and every time I win,
And if I ever have a son, I think I'm gonna name him
Bill or George! Anything but Sue! I still hate that name!

(a) Why is the songwriter angry in this song? Refer to the text in your answer.

(b) How does the songwriter feel about his father? Explain.

(c) Explain with reference to the text what happens when the father and son finally meet.

(d) Explain the father's reasons for naming his son 'Sue'.

(e) What feelings does this song evoke in you? Explain your answer with reference to the lyrics.

(f) Referring to both lyrics and music, explain why you think this song appeals to such a large audience.

(g) Explain why you like or don't like this song. Refer to both lyrics and music.

_____
_____
_____
_____
_____

3. Read the lyrics below and if possible listen to a recording of the song. Then answer the questions that follow.

Luka

My name is Luka
I live on the second floor
I live upstairs from you
Yes I think you've seen me before.

If you hear something late at night
Some kind of trouble, some kind of fight,
Just don't ask me what it was
Just don't ask me what it was
Just don't ask me what it was.

<u>I think it's because I'm clumsy</u>
<u>I try not to talk too loud</u>
<u>Maybe it's because I'm crazy</u>
<u>I try not to act too proud</u>

They only hit until you cry,
After that you don't ask why.
You just don't argue anymore
You just don't argue anymore
You just don't argue anymore.

Yes I think I'm okay,
I walked into the door again.
Well, if you ask that's what I'll say
And it's not your business, anyway.

I guess I'd like to be alone
With nothing broken, nothing thrown.

Just don't ask me how I am
Just don't ask me how I am
Just don't ask me how I am.

My name is Luka
I live on the second floor
I live upstairs from you
Yes I think you've seen me before.

If you hear something late at night
Some kind of trouble, some kind of fight,
Just don't ask me what it was
Just don't ask me what it was
Just don't ask me what it was.

And they only hit until you cry,
After that, you don't ask why.
You just don't argue anymore

You just don't argue anymore
You just don't argue anymore.

(a) Explain what is happening in this song.

___

(b) What is the main theme? Explain your answer.

___

(c) What is the atmosphere of this song? Refer in your answer to both the lyrics and the music.

___

(d) Looking at the lyrics only, what are the indications that they could be suitably set to music? Refer to rhyme, rhythm and repetition in your answer.

___

Module 4 – Critical Literacy and Composition

(e) Select an image from the lyrics that you found striking and explain why you think it is so effective.

_____
_____
_____
_____

(f) Look at the underlined section of this song. What does it mean?

_____
_____
_____
_____
_____
_____

(g) Why do you think this song would appeal to a large audience? Refer to both lyrics and music in your answer.

_____
_____
_____
_____
_____

(h) What is your opinion of this song? Comment on both the lyrics and the music.

_____
_____
_____
_____

Writing Your Own Song or Poem

STANDARD ASSIGNMENT

- **Study the lyrics of a songwriter or group that you like. Keep a record of your findings.**
- **Keep samples of some of your own creative writing, e.g. song lyrics or poetry.**

161

1. Think about a time in your life that caused you to feel very strong emotions, e.g. falling in love, getting angry at someone, being afraid, etc. Describe what happened.

2. What feelings were most dominant at that time? Why?

3. What metaphors or comparisons can you think of to help define your feelings at that time?

4. What techniques help to make a poem suitable to set to music?

5. Using your answers to Questions 1–4, write song lyrics or a short poem that reflects the feelings you had during a personal experience.

INCORPORATING I.T.

Type your song lyrics or poem using Microsoft Word or a similar program. Decorate the page with images that convey the feelings in your text. You can use Google Images to help you find something suitable. As a class group, you can then make a big poster to display all your hard work! ☺

ADVANCED ASSIGNMENT

Select a song that has particular meaning for you. Write an article for a magazine, explaining why you like the song. In your article, refer to the music, lyrics, artist, imagery, atmosphere, rhyme and rhythm.

INCORPORATING I.T.

Use a computer to type your article and remember to give it a suitable headline. You could add your finished article to the class poster of song lyrics.

CHAPTER 15 Poetry

1. Read the poem below and answer the questions that follow.

If

by Rudyard Kipling

If you can keep your head when all about you
    Are losing theirs and blaming it on you,
If you can trust yourself when all men doubt you,
    But make allowance for their doubting too;
If you can wait and not be tired by waiting,
    Or being lied about, don't deal in lies,
Or being hated, don't give way to hating,
    And yet don't look too good, nor talk too wise:

If you can dream – and not make dreams your master;
    If you can think – and not make thoughts your aim;
If you can meet with Triumph and Disaster
    And treat those two impostors just the same;
If you can bear to hear the truth you've spoken
    Twisted by knaves to make a trap for fools,
Or watch the things you gave your life to, broken,
    And stoop and build 'em up with worn-out tools:

If you can make one heap of all your winnings
    And risk it on one turn of pitch-and-toss,
And lose, and start again at your beginnings
    And never breathe a word about your loss;
If you can force your heart and nerve and sinew
    To serve your turn long after they are gone,
And so hold on when there is nothing in you
    Except the Will which says to them: 'Hold on!'

If you can talk with crowds and keep your virtue,
    Or walk with Kings – nor lose the common touch,
If neither foes nor loving friends can hurt you,
    If all men count with you, but none too much;
If you can fill the unforgiving minute
    With sixty seconds' worth of distance run,
Yours is the Earth and everything that's in it,
    And – which is more – you'll be a Man, my son!

Beat! LCA English Assignments Workbook

(a) What advice does the poet give his son in the first stanza of the poem?

(b) What advice does he give in the third stanza?

(c) What will be the outcome, according to the poet, if his son follows all his advice?

(d) What would you say is the overall theme of this poem?

(e) What is the mood of this poem?

(f) Comment on the following aspects of the poem:

- rhythm

- rhyme

- repetition

(g) How do you think the poet feels about his son?

(h) How do you think the son would react to all the advice his father gives him?

(i) Imagine you are the son mentioned in the poem. Write a poem in response to your father's advice.
Remember: you should try to use poetic techniques, such as rhyme, rhythm, imagery, etc.

2. Examine the two poems below. Read each poem twice, then answer the questions that follow.

"Hope" is the thing with feathers —
by Emily Dickinson

"Hope" is the thing with feathers —
That perches in the soul —
And sings the tune without the words —
And never stops — at all —

And sweetest — in the Gale — is heard —
And sore must be the storm —
That could abash the little Bird
That kept so many warm —

I've heard it in the chillest land —
And on the strangest Sea —
Yet, never, in Extremity,
It asked a crumb — of me.

Nothing Gold Can Stay
by Robert Frost

Nature's first green is gold
Her hardest hue to hold.
Her early leaf's a flower;
But only so an hour.
Then leaf subsides to leaf.
So Eden sank to grief,
So dawn goes down to day.
Nothing gold can stay.

"Hope" is the thing with feathers — *by Emily Dickinson*

(a) What is the central theme of this poem?

_____
_____
_____

(b) To what does Emily Dickinson compare hope? Do you think this is a good comparison (metaphor)? Explain.

_____
_____
_____
_____

(c) Explain the meaning of this poem.

_____
_____
_____

(d) Comment on the following aspects of the poem:

- rhythm

_____
_____

- rhyme

_____
_____

- repetition

_____
_____

(e) Choose one image that you particularly liked in the poem and say why it struck you.

_____
_____
_____

(f) Would you be interested in reading more of Emily Dickinson's poetry? Give reasons for your answer.

_____
_____
_____
_____

Nothing Gold Can Stay *by Robert Frost*

(a) What is the central theme of this poem?

(b) From your reading of this poem, would you regard Robert Frost as an optimist, pessimist or realist? Explain your answer.

(c) How would you describe the poet's **tone** in the final two lines?

(d) Explain the meaning of this poem.

(e) Comment on the following aspects of the poem:

- rhythm

- rhyme

- repetition

(f) Choose one image that you particularly liked in the poem and say why it struck you.

_____
_____
_____

(g) Would you be interested in reading more of Robert Frost's poetry? Give reasons for your answer.

_____
_____
_____

Comparing poems

1. Each of these poems deals with a similar theme in different ways. Compare each poet's treatment of the theme and then answer the questions below.

    (a) Which of the two poems did you prefer? Give reasons for your answer.

    _____
    _____

    (b) What are the main differences between each poet's treatment of the theme of hope?

    _____
    _____
    _____

    (c) Do the poets show any similarity in style? Refer to rhythm, rhyme, imagery, sound, etc.

    _____
    _____
    _____
    _____

    (d) Which poem do you think would have greater universal appeal?

    _____
    _____
    _____

STANDARD ASSIGNMENT

Conduct a close study of a range of contemporary poetry. Keep samples of some of your own creative writing in relation to poetry.

(e) Compose a short poem on the theme of hope. Try to use poetic techniques, such as rhyme, rhythm, imagery, etc.

_____
_____
_____
_____
_____
_____
_____
_____
_____
_____
_____
_____
_____
_____
_____
_____
_____
_____

INCORPORATING I.T.

Type your poem using Microsoft Word or a similar program. Use images from the Internet to decorate your poem and make a poster for your classroom wall! ☺

CHAPTER 16 Short Story

1. Below is the short story 'My Oedipus Complex' by Frank O'Connor. Read the short story and answer the questions that follow.

> Father was in the army all through the war – the First War, I mean – so, up to the age of five, I never saw much of him, and what I saw did not worry me. Sometimes I woke and there was a big figure in khaki peering down at me in the candlelight. Sometimes in the early morning I heard the slamming of the front door and the clatter of nailed boots down the cobbles of the lane. These were Father's entrances and exits. Like Santa Claus he came and went mysteriously.
>
> In fact, I rather liked his visits, though it was an uncomfortable squeeze between Mother and him when I got into the big bed in the early morning. He smoked, which gave him a pleasant musty smell, and shaved, an operation of astounding interest. Each time he left a trail of souvenirs – model tanks and Gurkha knives with handles made of bullet cases, and German helmets and cap badges and button-sticks, and all sorts of military equipment – carefully stowed away in a long box on top of the wardrobe, in case they ever came in handy. There was a bit of the magpie about Father; he expected everything to come in handy. When his back was turned, Mother let me get a chair and rummage through his treasures. She didn't seem to think so highly of them as he did.
>
> The war was the most peaceful period of my life. The window of my attic faced south-east. My mother had curtained it, but that had small effect. I always woke with the first light and, with all the responsibilities of the previous day melted, feeling myself rather like the sun, ready to illumine and rejoice. Life never seemed so simple and clear and full of possibilities as then. I put my feet out from under the clothes – I called them Mrs Left and Mrs Right – and invented dramatic situations for them in which they discussed the problems of the day. At least Mrs Right did; she was very demonstrative, but I hadn't the same control of Mrs Left, so she mostly contented herself with nodding agreement.
>
> They discussed what Mother and I should do during the day, what Santa Claus should give a fellow for Christmas, and what steps should be taken to brighten the home. There was that little matter of the baby, for instance. Mother and I could never agree about that. Ours was the only house in the terrace without a new baby, and Mother said we couldn't afford one till Father came back from the war because they cost seventeen and six. That showed how simple she was. The Geneys up the road had a baby, and everyone knew they couldn't afford seventeen and six. It was probably a cheap baby, and Mother wanted something really good, but I felt she was too exclusive. The Geneys' baby would have done us fine.

Having settled my plans for the day, I got up, put a chair under the attic window, and lifted the frame high enough to stick out my head. The window overlooked the front gardens of the terrace behind ours, and beyond these it looked over a deep valley to the tall, red-brick houses terraced up the opposite hillside, which were all still in shadow, while those at our side of the valley were all lit up, though with long strange shadows that made them seem unfamiliar; rigid and painted.

After that I went into Mother's room and climbed into the big bed. She woke and I began to tell her of my schemes. By this time, though I never seemed to have noticed it, I was petrified in my nightshirt, and I thawed as I talked until, the last frost melted, I fell asleep beside her and woke again only when I heard her below in the kitchen, making the breakfast.

After breakfast we went into town; heard Mass at St Augustine's and said a prayer for Father, and did the shopping. If the afternoon was fine we either went for a walk in the country or a visit to Mother's great friend in the convent, Mother St Dominic. Mother had them all praying for Father, and every night, going to bed, I asked God to send him back safe from the war to us. Little, indeed, did I know what I was praying for!

One morning I got into the big bed, and there, sure enough, was Father in his usual Santa Claus manner, but later, instead of uniform, he put on his best blue suit, and Mother was as pleased as anything. I saw nothing to be pleased about, because, out of uniform, Father was altogether less interesting, but she only beamed, and explained that our prayers had been answered, and off we went to Mass to thank God for having brought Father safely home.

The irony of it! That very day when he came in to dinner he took off his boots and put on his slippers, donned the dirty old cap he wore about the house to save him from colds, crossed his legs, and began to talk gravely to Mother, who looked anxious. Naturally, I disliked her looking anxious, because it destroyed her good looks, so I interrupted him.

'Just a moment, Larry!' she said gently.

This was only what she said when we had boring visitors, so I attached no importance to it and went on talking.

'Do be quiet, Larry!' she said impatiently. 'Don't you hear me talking to Daddy?'

This was the first time I had heard those ominous words, 'talking to Daddy', and I couldn't help feeling that if this was how God answered prayers, he couldn't listen to them very attentively.

'Why are you talking to Daddy?' I asked with as great a show of indifference as I could muster.

'Because Daddy and I have business to discuss. Now, don't interrupt again!'

In the afternoon, at Mother's request, Father took me for a walk. This time we went into town instead of out in the country, and I thought at first, in my usual optimistic way, that it might be an improvement. It was nothing of the sort. Father and I had quite different notions of a walk in town. He had no proper interest in trams, ships, and horses, and the only thing that seemed to divert him was talking to fellows as old as himself. When I wanted to stop he simply went on, dragging me behind him by the hand; when he wanted to stop I had no alternative but to do the same. I noticed that it seemed to be a sign that he wanted to stop for a long time whenever he leaned against a wall. The second time I saw him do it I got wild. He seemed to be settling himself forever. I pulled him by the coat and trousers, but, unlike Mother who, if you were too persistent, got into a wax and said: 'Larry, if you don't behave yourself, I'll give you a good slap,' Father had an extraordinary capacity for amiable inattention. I sized him up and wondered would I cry, but he seemed to be too remote to be annoyed even by that. Really, it was like going for a walk with a mountain! He either ignored the wrenching and pummelling entirely, or else glanced down with a grin of amusement from his peak. I had never met anyone so absorbed in himself as he seemed.

At teatime, 'talking to Daddy' began again, complicated this time by the fact that he had an evening paper, and every few minutes he put it down and told Mother something new out of it. I felt this was foul play. Man for man, I was prepared to compete with him any time for Mother's attention, but when he had it all made up for him by other people it left me no chance. Several times I tried to change the subject without success.

'You must be quiet while Daddy is reading, Larry,' Mother said impatiently.

It was clear that she either genuinely liked talking to Father better than talking to me, or else that he had some terrible hold on her which made her afraid to admit the truth.

'Mummy,' I said that night when she was tucking me up, 'do you think if I prayed hard God would send Daddy back to the war?'

She seemed to think about that for a moment.

'No, dear,' she said with a smile. 'I don't think he would.'

'Why wouldn't he, Mummy?'

'Because there isn't a war any longer, dear.'

'But, Mummy, couldn't God make another war, if he liked?'

'He wouldn't like to, dear. It's not God who makes wars, but bad people.'

'Oh!' I said.

I was disappointed about that. I began to think that God wasn't quite what he was cracked up to be.

Next morning I woke at my usual hour, feeling like a bottle of champagne. I put out my feet and invented a long conversation in which Mrs Right talked of the trouble she had with her own father till she put him in the Home. I didn't quite know what the Home was but it sounded the right place for Father. Then I got my chair and stuck my head out of the attic window. Dawn was just breaking, with a guilty air that made me feel I had caught it in the act. My head bursting with stories and schemes, I stumbled in next door, and in the half-darkness scrambled into the big bed. There was no room at Mother's side so I had to get between her and Father. For the time being I had forgotten about him, and for several minutes I sat bolt upright, racking my brains to know what I could do with him. He was taking up more than his fair share of the bed, and I couldn't get comfortable, so I gave him several kicks that made him grunt and stretch. He made room all right, though. Mother waked and felt for me. I settled back comfortably in the warmth of the bed with my thumb in my mouth.

'Mummy!' I hummed, loudly and contentedly.

'Sssh! dear,' she whispered. 'Don't wake Daddy!'

This was a new development, which threatened to be even more serious than 'talking to Daddy'. Life without my early-morning conferences was unthinkable.

'Why?' I asked severely.

'Because poor Daddy is tired.'

This seemed to me a quite inadequate reason, and I was sickened by the sentimentality of her 'poor Daddy'. I never liked that sort of gush; it always struck me as insincere.

'Oh!' I said lightly. Then in my most winning tone: 'Do you know where I want to go with you today, Mummy?'

'No, dear,' she sighed.

'I want to go down the Glen and fish for thornybacks with my new net, and then I want to go out to the Fox and Hounds, and –'

'Don't-wake-Daddy!' she hissed angrily, clapping her hand across my mouth.

But it was too late. He was awake, or nearly so. He grunted and reached for the matches. Then he stared incredulously at his watch.

'Like a cup of tea, dear?' asked Mother in a meek, hushed voice I had never heard her use before. It sounded almost as though she were afraid.

'Tea?' he exclaimed indignantly. 'Do you know what the time is?'

'And after that I want to go up the Rathcooney Road,' I said loudly, afraid I'd forget something in all those interruptions.

'Go to sleep at once, Larry!' she said sharply.

I began to snivel. I couldn't concentrate, the way that pair went on, and smothering my early-morning schemes was like burying a family from the cradle.

Father said nothing, but lit his pipe and sucked it, looking out into the shadows without minding Mother or me. I knew he was mad. Every time I made a remark Mother hushed me irritably. I was mortified. I felt it wasn't fair; there was even something sinister in it. Every time I had pointed out to her the waste of making two beds when we could both sleep in one, she had told me it was healthier like that, and now here was this man, this stranger, sleeping with her without the least regard for her health!

He got up early and made tea, but though he brought Mother a cup he brought none for me.

'Mummy,' I shouted, 'I want a cup of tea, too.'

'Yes, dear,' she said patiently. 'You can drink from Mummy's saucer.'

That settled it. Either Father or I would have to leave the house. I didn't want to drink from Mother's saucer; I wanted to be treated as an equal in my own home, so, just to spite her, I drank it all and left none for her. She took that quietly, too.

But that night when she was putting me to bed she said gently:

'Larry, I want you to promise me something.'

'What is it?' I asked.

'Not to come in and disturb poor Daddy in the morning. Promise?'

'Poor Daddy' again! I was becoming suspicious of everything involving that quite impossible man.

'Why?' I asked.

'Because poor Daddy is worried and tired and he doesn't sleep well.'

'Why doesn't he, Mummy?'

'Well, you know, don't you, that while he was at the war Mummy got the pennies from the Post Office?'

'From Miss MacCarthy?'

'That's right. But now, you see, Miss MacCarthy hasn't any more pennies, so Daddy must go out and find us some. You know what would happen if he couldn't?'

'No,' I said, 'tell us.'

'Well, I think we might have to go out and beg for them like the poor old woman on Fridays. We wouldn't like that, would we?'

'No,' I agreed. 'We wouldn't.'

'So you'll promise not to come in and wake him?'

'Promise.'

Mind you, I meant that. I knew pennies were a serious matter, and I was all against having to go out and beg like the old woman on Fridays. Mother laid out all my toys in a complete ring round the bed so that, whatever way I got out, I was bound to fall over one of them.

When I woke I remembered my promise all right. I got up and sat on the floor and played – for hours, it seemed to me. Then I got my chair and looked out the attic window for more hours. I wished it was time for Father to wake; I wished someone would make me a cup of tea. I didn't feel in the least like the sun; instead, I was bored and so very, very cold! I simply longed for the warmth and depth of the big featherbed.

At last I could stand it no longer. I went into the next room. As there was still no room at Mother's side I climbed over her and she woke with a start.

'Larry,' she whispered, gripping my arm very tightly, 'what did you promise?'

'But I did, Mummy,' I wailed, caught in the very act. 'I was quiet for ever so long.'

'Oh, dear, and you're perished!' she said sadly, feeling me all over. 'Now, if I let you stay will you promise not to talk?'

'But I want to talk, Mummy,' I wailed.

'That has nothing to do with it,' she said with a firmness that was new to me. 'Daddy wants to sleep. Now, do you understand that?'

I understood it only too well. I wanted to talk, he wanted to sleep – whose house was it, anyway?

'Mummy,' I said with equal firmness, 'I think it would be healthier for Daddy to sleep in his own bed.'

That seemed to stagger her, because she said nothing for a while.

'Now, once for all,' she went on, 'you're to be perfectly quiet or go back to your own bed. Which is it to be?'

The injustice of it got me down. I had convicted her out of her own mouth of inconsistency and unreasonableness, and she hadn't even attempted to reply. Full of spite, I gave Father a kick, which she didn't notice but which made him grunt and open his eyes in alarm.

'What time is it?' he asked in a panic-stricken voice, not looking at Mother but at the door, as if he saw someone there.

'It's early yet,' she replied soothingly. 'It's only the child. Go to sleep again... Now, Larry,' she added, getting out of bed, 'you've wakened Daddy and you must go back.'

This time, for all her quiet air, I knew she meant it, and knew that my principal rights and privileges were as good as lost unless I asserted them at once. As she lifted me, I gave a screech, enough to wake the dead, not to mind Father. He groaned.

'That damn child! Doesn't he ever sleep?'

'It's only a habit, dear,' she said quietly, though I could see she was vexed.

'Well, it's time he got out of it,' shouted Father, beginning to heave in the bed. He suddenly gathered all the bedclothes about him, turned to the wall, and then looked back over his shoulder with nothing showing only two small, spiteful, dark eyes. The man looked very wicked.

To open the bedroom door, Mother had to let me down, and I broke free and dashed for the farthest corner, screeching. Father sat bolt upright in bed.

'Shut up, you little puppy!' he said in a choking voice.

I was so astonished that I stopped screeching. Never, never had anyone spoken to me in that tone before. I looked at him incredulously and saw his face convulsed with rage. It was only then that I fully realized how God had codded me, listening to my prayers for the safe return of this monster.

'Shut up, you!' I bawled, beside myself.

'What's that you said?' shouted Father, making a wild leap out of the bed.

'Mick, Mick!' cried Mother. 'Don't you see the child isn't used to you?'

'I see he's better fed than taught,' snarled Father, waving his arms wildly. 'He wants his bottom smacked.'

All his previous shouting was as nothing to these obscene words referring to my person. They really made my blood boil.

'Smack your own!' I screamed hysterically. 'Smack your own! Shut up! Shut up!'

At this he lost his patience and let fly at me. He did it with the lack of conviction you'd expect of a man under Mother's horrified eyes, and it ended up as a mere tap, but the sheer indignity of being struck at all by a stranger, a total stranger who had cajoled his way back from the war into our big bed as a result of my innocent intercession, made me completely dotty. I shrieked and shrieked, and danced in my bare feet, and Father, looking awkward and hairy in nothing but a short grey army shirt, glared down at me like a mountain out for murder. I think it must have been then that I realized he was jealous too. And there stood Mother in her nightdress, looking as if her heart was broken between us. I hoped she felt as she looked. It seemed to me that she deserved it all.

From that morning out my life was a hell. Father and I were enemies, open and avowed. We conducted a series of skirmishes against one another, he trying to steal my time with Mother and I his. When she was sitting on my bed, telling me a story, he took to looking for some pair of old boots which he alleged he had left behind him at the beginning of the war. While he talked to Mother I played loudly with my toys to show my total lack of concern. He created a terrible scene one evening when he came in from work and found me at his box, playing with his regimental badges, Gurkha knives and button-sticks. Mother got up and took the box from me.

'You mustn't play with Daddy's toys unless he lets you, Larry,' she said severely. 'Daddy doesn't play with yours.'

For some reason Father looked at her as if she had struck him and then turned away with a scowl.

'Those are not toys,' he growled, taking down the box again to see had I lifted anything. 'Some of those curios are very rare and valuable.'

But as time went on I saw more and more how he managed to alienate Mother and me. What made it worse was that I couldn't grasp his method or see what attraction he had for Mother. In every possible way he was less winning than I. He had a common accent and made noises at his tea. I thought for a while that it might be the newspapers she was interested in, so I made up bits of news of my own to read to her. Then I thought it might be the smoking, which I personally thought attractive, and took his pipes and went round the house dribbling into them till he caught me. I even made noises at my tea, but Mother only told me I was disgusting. It all seemed to hinge round that unhealthy habit of sleeping together, so I made a point of dropping into their bedroom and nosing round, talking to myself, so that they wouldn't know I was watching them, but they were never up to anything that I could see. In the end it beat me. It seemed to depend on being grown-up and giving people rings, and I realized I'd have to wait.

But at the same time I wanted him to see that I was only waiting, not giving up the fight. One evening when he was being particularly obnoxious, chattering away well above my head, I let him have it.

'Mummy,' I said, 'do you know what I'm going to do when I grow up?'

'No, dear,' she replied. 'What?'

'I'm going to marry you,' I said quietly.

Father gave a great guffaw out of him, but he didn't take me in. I knew it must only be pretence. And Mother, in spite of everything, was pleased. I felt she was probably relieved to know that one day Father's hold on her would be broken.

'Won't that be nice?' she said with a smile.

'It'll be very nice,' I said confidently. 'Because we're going to have lots and lots of babies.'

'That's right, dear,' she said placidly. 'I think we'll have one soon, and then you'll have plenty of company.'

I was no end pleased about that because it showed that in spite of the way she gave in to Father she still considered my wishes. Besides, it would put the Geneys in their place.

It didn't turn out like that, though. To begin with, she was very preoccupied – I supposed about where she would get the seventeen and six – and though Father took to staying out late in the evenings it did me no particular good. She stopped taking me for walks, became as touchy as blazes, and smacked me for nothing at all. Sometimes I wished I'd never mentioned the confounded baby – I seemed to have a genius for bringing calamity on myself.

And calamity it was! Sonny arrived in the most appalling hullabaloo – even that much he couldn't do without a fuss – and from the first moment I disliked him. He was a difficult child – so far as I was concerned he was always difficult – and demanded far too much attention. Mother was simply silly about him, and couldn't see when he was only showing off. As company he was worse than useless. He slept all day, and I had to go round the house on tiptoe to avoid waking him. It wasn't any longer a question of not waking Father. The slogan now was 'Don't-wake-Sonny!' I couldn't understand why the child wouldn't sleep at the proper time, so whenever Mother's back was turned I woke him. Sometimes to keep him awake I pinched him as well. Mother caught me at it one day and gave me a most unmerciful flaking.

One evening, when Father was coming in from work, I was playing trains in the front garden. I let on not to notice him; instead, I pretended to be talking to myself, and said in a loud voice: 'If another bloody baby comes into this house, I'm going out.'

Father stopped dead and looked at me over his shoulder.

'What's that you said?' he asked sternly.

'I was only talking to myself,' I replied, trying to conceal my panic. 'It's private.'

He turned and went in without a word. Mind you, I intended it as a solemn warning, but its effect was quite different. Father started being quite nice to me. I could understand that, of course. Mother was quite sickening about Sonny. Even at mealtimes she'd get up and gawk at him in the cradle with an idiotic smile, and tell Father to do the same. He was always polite about it, but he looked so puzzled you could see he didn't know what she was talking about. He complained of the way Sonny cried at night, but she only got cross and said that Sonny never cried except when there was something up with him – which was a flaming lie, because Sonny never had anything up with him, and only cried for attention. It was really painful to see how simpleminded she was. Father wasn't attractive, but he had a fine intelligence. He saw through Sonny, and now he knew that I saw through him as well. One night I woke with a start. There was someone beside me in the bed. For one wild moment I felt sure it must be Mother, having come to her senses and left Father for good, but then I heard Sonny in convulsions in the next room, and Mother saying: 'There! There! There!' and I knew it wasn't she. It was Father. He was lying beside me, wide awake, breathing hard and apparently as mad as hell.

After a while it came to me what he was mad about. It was his turn now. After turning me out of the big bed, he had been turned out himself. Mother had no consideration now for anyone but that poisonous pup, Sonny. I couldn't help feeling sorry for Father. I had been through it all myself, and even at that age I was magnanimous. I began to stroke him down and say: 'There! There!' He wasn't exactly responsive.

'Aren't you asleep either?' he snarled.

'Ah, come on and put your arm around us, can't you?' I said, and he did, in a sort of way. Gingerly, I suppose, is how you'd describe it. He was very bony but better than nothing.

At Christmas he went out of his way to buy me a really nice model railway.

(a) Describe the setting of this story.

(b) Why was Larry's father so rarely at home? How did Larry feel about this?

(c) Larry asks his mother if they can get a baby. What reason does she give for refusing?

(d) When the war ended, Larry's world changed dramatically. Describe these changes and explain the causes.

_____

_____

_____

_____

(e) How did the father in the story feel about his son, Larry? Explain your answer.

_____

_____

_____

(f) Larry's relationship with his father changed towards the end of the story. Explain the reason for this.

_____

_____

_____

(g) What would you say is the main theme of this story?

_____

_____

_____

(h) Describe the plot.

_____

_____

_____

_____

_____

_____

_____

_____

(i) What kind of person would you say Larry is?

(j) At what stage does the story reach the climax? Explain your answer.

(k) Larry is a young boy in the story. Would you say the language in the story suits him? Why do you think the author uses this style of language?

(l) Retell this story from the mother's point of view.

(m) What do you think are the most important elements that make a good short story? Explain your answer.

(n) In your opinion, what are the main differences between the short story form and the novel form?

Creative Writing

STANDARD ASSIGNMENT

Conduct a close study of one writer of short stories.

ADVANCED ASSIGNMENT

Try some creative writing yourself and keep samples of your work.

Write a review

2. Revise Chapter 5: Writing a Review, then write a review of 'My Oedipus Complex' by Frank O'Connor for your school magazine.

Keep in mind the following questions when writing reviews:

- Briefly explain the plot.
- How well did the writer create the setting and the characters?
- Who was the main character? Was he or she likeable or unpleasant? Why?
- What elements of the story did you enjoy?
- What parts of the story do you feel could have been improved or adapted?
- Overall, did you enjoy the short story? Would you recommend it to others?

INCORPORATING I.T.

Use a computer to type your review and present it to your teacher. 🙂

CHAPTER 17 Novel

> ✓ **Useful TIP!**
>
> For this chapter the novel selected is John Steinbeck's *Of Mice and Men*. While an extract appears below, it is recommended that you read the entire text.

1. Read the extract from *Of Mice and Men* by John Steinbeck and answer the questions that follow.

A few miles south of Soledad, the Salinas River drops in close to the hillside bank and runs deep and green. The water is warm too, for it has slipped twinkling over the yellow sands in the sunlight before reaching the narrow pool. On one side of the river the golden foothill slopes curve up to the strong and rocky Gablian mountains, but on the valley side the water is lined with trees – willows fresh and green with every spring, carrying in their lower leaf junctures the debris of the winter's flooding; and sycamores with mottled, white, recumbent limbs and branches that arch over the pool. On the sandy bank under the trees the leaves lie deep and so crisp that a lizard makes a great skittering if he runs among them. Rabbits come out of the brush to sit on the sand in the evening, and the damp flats are covered with the night tracks of 'coons, and with the spread pads of dogs from the ranches, and with the split-wedge tracks of deer that come to drink in the dark.

There is a path through the willows and among the sycamores, a path beaten hard by boys coming down from the ranches to swim in the deep pool, and beaten hard by tramps who come wearily down from the highway in the evening to jungle-up near water. In front of the low horizontal limb of a giant sycamore there is an ash pile made by many fires; the limb is worn smooth by men who have sat on it.

Evening of a hot day started the little wind to moving among the leaves. The shade climbed up the hills toward the top. On the sand banks the rabbits sat as quietly as little gray sculpture stones. And then from the direction of the state highway came the sound of footsteps on crisp sycamore leaves. The rabbits hurried noiselessly for cover. A stilted heron laboured up into the air and pounded down river. For a moment the place was lifeless, and then two men emerged from the path and came into the opening by the green pool.

They had walked in single file down the path, and even in the open one stayed behind the other. Both were dressed in denim trousers and in denim coats with brass buttons. Both wore black, shapeless hats and both carried tight blanket rolls slung over their shoulders. The first man was small and quick, dark of face, with restless eyes and sharp strong features. Every part of him was defined: small, strong hands, slender arms, a thin and bony nose. Behind him walked his opposite, a huge man, shapeless of face, with large, pale eyes, with wide, sloping shoulders; and he walked heavily, dragging his feet a little, the way a bear drags his paws. His arms did not swing at his sides, but hung loosely.

The first man stopped short in the clearing, and the follower nearly ran over him. He took off his hat and wiped the sweat-band with his forefinger and snapped the moisture off. His huge companion dropped his blankets and flung himself down from the surface of the green pool; drank with long gulps, snorting into the water like a horse. The small man stepped nervously behind him.

'Lennie!' he said sharply. 'Lennie, for God' sakes don't drink so much.' Lennie continued to snort into the pool. The small man leaned over and shook him by the shoulder. 'Lennie. You gonna be sick like you was last night.'

Lennie dipped his whole head under, hat and all, and then he sat up on the bank and his hat dripped down on his blue coat and ran down his back. 'Tha's good,' he said. 'You drink some George. You take a good big drink.' He smiled happily.

George unslung his bindle and dropped it gently on the bank. 'I ain't sure it's good water,' he said. 'Looks kinda scummy.'

<u>Lennie dabbled his big paw in the water and wiggled his fingers so the water arose in little splashes; rings widened across the pool to the other side and came back again. Lennie watched them go. 'Look, George. Look what I done.'</u>

George knelt beside the pool and drank from his hand with quick scoops. 'Tastes all right,' he admitted. 'Don't really seem to be running, though. You never oughta drink water when it ain't running, Lennie,' he said hopelessly. 'You'd drink out of a gutter if you was thirsty.' He threw a scoop of water into his face and rubbed it about with his hand, under his chin and around the back of his neck. Then he replaced his hat, pushed himself back, drew up his knees and embraced them. Lennie, who had been watching, imitated George exactly. He pushed himself back, drew up his knees, embraced them, and looked over to George to see whether he had it just right. He pulled his hat down a little more over his eyes, the way George's hat was.

George stared morosely at the water. The rims of his eyes were red with sun glare. He said angrily, 'We could just as well of rode clear to the ranch if that bus driver knew what he was talkin' about. "Jes' a little stretch." God damn near four miles, that's what it was! Didn't wanta stop at the ranch gate, that's what. Too god damn lazy to pull up. Kicks us out and says, "Jes' a little stretch down the road." I bet it was *more* than four miles. Damn hot day.'

Lennie looked timidly over to him. 'George?'

'Yeah, what ya want?'

'Where we goin' George?'

The little man jerked down the brim of his hat and scowled over at Lennie. 'So you forgot that awready, did you? I gotta tell you again, do I? Jesus Christ, you're crazy.'

'I forgot,' Lennie said softly. 'I tried not to forget. Honest to God I did, George.'

'O.K. – O.K. I'll tell ya again. I ain't got nothing to do. Might jus' as well spen' all my time tellin' you things and then you forget 'em and I tell you again.'

'Tried and tried,' said Lennie, 'but it didn't do no good. I remember about the rabbits, George.'

'The hell with the rabbits. That's all you ever can remember is them rabbits. O.K.! Now you listen and this time you got to remember so we don't get in no trouble. You remember settin' in that gutter on Howard Street and watchin' that blackboard?'

Lennie's face broke into a delighted smile. 'Why sure, George, I remember that…but…what'd we do then? I remember some girls come by and you says…you say…'

'The hell with what I says. You remember about us going' into Murray and Ready's, and they give us work cards and bus tickets?'

'Oh, sure, George. I remember that now.' His hands went quickly into his side coat pockets. He said gently, 'George…I ain't got mine. I musta lost it.' He looked down at the ground in despair.

'You never had none. I got both of 'em here. Think I'd let you carry your own work card?'

Lennie grinned with relief. 'I…I thought I put it in my side pocket.' His hand went into the pocket again.

George looked sharply at him. 'What'd you take outta that pocket?'

'Ain't a thing in my pocket,' Lennie said cleverly.

'I know there ain't. You got it in your hand. What you got in your hand – hidin' it?'

'I ain't got nothin', George. Honest.'

'Come on, give it here.'

Lennie held his closed hand away from George's direction. 'It's on'y a mouse, George.'

'A mouse? A live mouse?'

'Uh-uh. Jus' a dead mouse, George. I didn't kill it. Honest! I found it. I found it dead.'

'Give it here!' said George.

'Aw, leave me have it George.'

'Give it here!'

Lennie's closed hand slowly obeyed. George took the mouse and threw it across the pool to the other side, among the brush. 'What you want of a dead mouse, anyways?'

'I could pet it with my thumb while we walked along,' said Lennie.

'Well, you ain't petting no mice while you walk with me. You remember where we're goin' now?'

Lennie looked startled and then in embarrassment hid his face against his knees. 'I forgot again.'

'Jesus Christ,' George said resignedly. 'Well – look we're gonna work on a ranch like the one we come from up north.'

'Up north?'

'In Weed.'

'Oh sure. I remember. In Weed.'

> 'That ranch we're goin' to is right down there about a quarter mile. We're gonna go in an' see the boss. Now, look – I'll give him the work tickets, but you ain't gonna say a word. You jus' stand there and don't say nothing. If he finds out how crazy you are, we won't get no job, but if he sees ya work before he hears ya talk, we're set. Ya got that?'
>
> 'Sure, George. Sure I got it.'
>
> 'O.K. Now when we go in to see the boss, what you gonna do?'
>
> 'I...I,' Lennie thought. His face grew tight with thought. 'I...ain't gonna say nothin'. Jus' gonna stan' there.'
>
> 'Good boy. That's swell. You say that over, two, three times so you sure won't forget it.'
>
> Lennie droned to himself softly, 'I ain't gonna say nothin'...ain't gonna say nothin'...I ain't gonna say nothin'.'
>
> 'O.K.,' said George. 'An' you ain't gonna do no bad things like you done in Weed, neither.'
>
> Lennie looked puzzled. 'Like I done in Weed?'
>
> 'Oh yeah, so you forgot that too, did ya? Well I ain't gonna remind ya, fear you do it again.'
>
> A light of understanding broke on Lennie's face. 'They run us outta Weed,' he exploded triumphantly.
>
> 'Run us out, hell,' said George disgustedly. 'We run. They was lookin' for us, but they didn't catch us...'

(a) Look at the first two paragraphs of this extract. Describe the opening setting in your own words.

_____

_____

_____

_____

_____

_____

_____

_____

(b) In what time period do you think this novel is set? Explain your answer.

_____

_____

_____

(c) Using the Internet, find a picture that you think shows a suitable setting for a film version of this novel. Print the picture and stick it into the box below. Alternatively, draw a sketch of a suitable setting.

(d) In the fourth paragraph we are given a description of two men, George and Lennie. Describe the men. If you were making a film version of this novel, what costume would you use for each of the men? Explain your choices.

_____
_____
_____
_____
_____

(e) Examine the underlined section of the extract. From this part of the text, describe the kind of person you think Lennie is. Give reasons for your answer.

_____
_____
_____
_____

(f) George is clearly the person in charge in this relationship. Choose a sentence in the text that shows this. Explain your choice.

_____
_____
_____
_____
_____
_____

(g) Give two reasons why the men are on foot and heading to a new ranch.

○ _____
_____

○ _____
_____

(h) Lennie doesn't seem to think before he acts. Where is this evident in the extract?

_____
_____
_____
_____

(i) In the last section of this extract we find that Lennie and George were 'run outta Weed'. What do you imagine might be the reason they were run out of town?

_____
_____
_____
_____

(j) What do you think will happen in the rest of the novel?

_____
_____
_____
_____

STANDARD ASSIGNMENT

Conduct a close study of a novel, or extracts from a novel. Keep one or more samples of your own creative writing.

2. Imagine that you are George. Write his description of what life is like looking after someone like Lennie.

ADVANCED ASSIGNMENT

Watch a film version of a novel you have read. Compare each version of the same story.

3. Watch the 1992 film version of *Of Mice and Men* on DVD. Compare the film to the novel. Use the questions below as a guide for your comparison.

    (a) How do the actors interpret their roles?

    _____
    _____
    _____
    _____

    (b) Describe how the setting of the film is similar or different from the novel.

    _____
    _____
    _____
    _____

    (c) What effects do the music and sound effects have on the film? Does this make it better than the novel?

    _____
    _____
    _____
    _____

    (d) Did you prefer the novel or the film? Explain your answer.

    _____
    _____
    _____
    _____

4. Using your answers to Question 3, write a **report** on your comparison of the novel *Of Mice and Men* and the 1992 film version. The template below will be useful.

Title: _____

Purpose: _____

_____

_____

_____

_____

Findings: _____

_____

_____

_____

_____

_____

_____

_____

_____

_____

Conclusions: _____

_____

_____

_____

_____

_____

_____

INCORPORATING I.T.

Use a computer to type your report and present it to your teacher. ☺

Studying a Novel of Your Choice

(a) Choose a novel that you have read. Give the title and the author.

_____
_____

(b) To what genre does the novel belong?

_____
_____

(c) Briefly outline the plot.

_____
_____
_____
_____
_____
_____

(d) Describe the setting.

_____
_____
_____

(e) Identify some of the elements that you believe helped to make this a good novel.

_____
_____
_____
_____

(f) Describe conflict that occurred in the novel.

_____
_____
_____

(g) Describe in detail the main character.

(h) Imagine you were creating a film version of this novel. Describe the costume, from head to toe, that you would select for the main character, giving reasons for each item of clothing.

(i) After reading this novel, would you be interested in reading more novels by this author? Why? Why not?

CHAPTER 18 Drama and Theatre

Television Drama

Only Fools and Horses is a well-known British sitcom that ran for seven series on BBC Television. Derek 'Del Boy' Trotter is a fast-talking market trader from a council flat in Nelson Mandela House in Peckham, London. The comedy focuses mainly on his futile attempts to get rich quick. In this extract, which was run as a five-minute special on a breakfast-time BBC programme in 1985, Del Boy has sold some white mice to a man, promising that they would turn into white horses at midnight. The following day, a representative from the BBC has come to investigate his claims.

1. Read the extract below and answer the questions that follow.

   Exterior, market. Del is stood beside his suitcase, which is full of handkerchiefs.

   Del: Come on, girls, come on. These are the finest handkerchiefs money can buy. Look at that, they're a pleasure to have the flu with, these.
   (Blows his nose into one) See that? They're lovely, they work, they're beautiful, now come on. Take 'em off me, listen, I gotta knock them out cause I want to get home early.

   A Woman, carrying a cage with six white mice, heads towards Del.

   Woman: Hello, are you Mr Trotter?

   Del: Yep, that's right darlin'. 'Ere you are, three for a pound.

   Woman: I don't want handkerchiefs. I want to talk to you about white mice.

   Del: White mice? Ah, that's a shame. You should have come yesterday. I had six beauties yesterday, but I sold them to a wally in a funny hat.

   Woman: That is exactly what I have come to see you about. My name is Lynne Faulds Wood.

   Del: Ah well, don't feel guilty about it girl, wasn't your fault, was it? Actually, Lynne happens to be my most favourite name. *(Del kisses her hand)*

   Woman: That's what they all say.

   Del: *(Still holding her hand)* My name is Del, short for Derek. *(Looks at her ring)* How much did you pay for that?

   Woman: *(Pulls her hand away)* Stop trying to change the subject!

   Del: I'm just saying that I could have got it cheaper for you. Do you like curry?

Woman:	Look, I'm Lynne Faulds Wood from the BBC's breakfast time programme, and I have come to see you because I have had a very serious complaint.
Del:	Complaint? Ah, no. Sorry, you have got the wrong department. I don't handle complaints. You have to see my Director of Public Relations. He's out at the moment. He's down at the café getting a bacon roll.
Woman:	Are you sure he's not stocking up on pork pies? Mr Trotter, you are the man I want to see. Now, yesterday afternoon you sold these six white mice to a Mr Buttons.
Del:	Mr Buttons? No, no, I told yer, I flogged 'em to a wally in a funny hat.
Woman:	Mr Buttons *IS* the wally in the funny hat! Now, you assured Mr Buttons that these white mice were magic, and that they would turn into horses.
Del:	*(Amused)* Did I say that?
Woman:	You most certainly did.
Del:	Turn into horses?
Woman:	Yes. And I am here to tell you, Mr Trotter that, surprise surprise, these white mice did not turn into horses.
Del:	Really? Now that does surprise me, that. 'Cause I have yet to have a white mouse that didn't turn into a horse. I mean, remember Red Rum? Well, I knew him when he was White Rum and used to run around in one of those little wheels.
Woman:	I have never heard such rubbish!
Del:	Well, hang about, I ain't finished yet.
Woman:	Oh, you will be, Mr Trotter, you will be when I have finished with you. Now you guaranteed Mr Buttons that these white mice would turn into horses at midnight. Look, they've patently failed. So, what are you going to do about it?
Del:	Oh, hang on, hang on! That wally Buttons never mentioned nothing about midnight, did he?
Woman:	What difference does the time make, anyway?
Del:	What difference? It makes a hell of a difference, 'cause these white mice are Korean.
Woman:	Korean?
Del:	Yeah.
Woman:	So what?
Del:	What do you mean, so what? You gotta take into consideration the international time difference. These white mice are still set to Korean time, ain't they? Hang about, look. *(Pulls out a calculator, works something out)* There, look at that. Now listen, you keep your eye on those white mice, 3.25 this afternoon, Bob's your uncle. You'll have more horses than Lester Piggott. Now, I must dash, 'cause I gotta see a bloke about a lamb. Ta-ra.

(a) What is Del selling at the beginning of the extract?

(b) What strategy does he use to sell his product?

(c) What strategy does Del use to try to avoid dealing with the woman's complaint?

(d) What evidence is there in the extract that Del is always looking for a new business venture?

(e) From your reading of the extract, describe Del's character.

(f) This episode was set in an open-air market. Imagine you are designing a set for a stage performance of this episode. Write out a description of what your set would look like.

(g) Draw your set design below.

(h) Describe the costume you would have Del wear for this scene and explain your choices.

_____
_____
_____
_____
_____
_____

(i) What sort of costume would the woman wear in this scene? Explain your answer.

_____
_____
_____
_____
_____
_____

(j) Comment on the dialogue in the extract. What does it say about the characters?

(k) Sound effects are an important part in making a scene believable. What sound effects could you include in a production of this scene? Explain your answer.

(l) Imagine you are interviewing the writer of this series for your school magazine. Write out five questions you would ask him or her.

-
-
-
-
-

(m) Imagine you are Del. You have returned home to your flat and are telling your brother Rodney about the incident in the market. Write out the conversation between you and Rodney. (Remember to use appropriate dialogue.)

Stage Drama

The Playboy of the Western World by J.M. Synge is a three-act play set in a small country pub in rural Mayo in the early 1900s.

2. Read the extract below and answer the questions that follow.

Country public-house or shebeen, very rough and untidy. There is a sort of counter on the right with shelves, holding many bottles and jugs, just seen above it. Empty barrels stand near the counter. At back, a little to the left of the counter, there is a door into the open air, then, more to the left, there is a settle with shelves above it, with more jugs, and a table beneath a window. At the left there is a large open fire-place, with turf fire, and a small door into inner room. Pegeen, a wild looking but fine girl, of about twenty, is writing at table. She is dressed in the usual peasant dress.

Pegeen: (*Slowly as she writes*) Six yards of stuff for to make a yellow gown. A pair of lace boots with lengthy heels on them and brassy eyes. A hat is suited for a wedding-day. A fine tooth comb. To be sent with three barrels of porter in Jimmy Farrell's creel cart on the evening of the coming Fair to Mister Michael James Flaherty. With the best compliments of this season. Margaret Flaherty.

Shawn: (*a fat and fair young man comes in as she signs, looks round awkwardly, when he sees she is alone.*) Where's himself?

Pegeen: (*without looking at him*) He's coming. (*She directs the letter*) To Mister Sheamus Mulroy, Wine and Spirit Dealer, Castlebar.

Shawn: (*uneasily*) I didn't see him on the road.

Pegeen: How would you see him (*licks stamp and puts it on letter*) and it dark night this half hour gone by?

Shawn: (*turning towards the door again*) I stood a while outside wondering would I have a right to pass on or to walk in and see you, Pegeen Mike (*comes to fire*), and I could hear the cows breathing, and sighing in the stillness of the air, and not a step moving any place from this gate to the bridge.

Pegeen: (*putting letter in envelope*) It's above at the cross-roads he is, meeting Philly Cullen; and a couple more are going along with him to Kate Cassidy's wake.

Shawn: (*looking at her blankly*) And he's going that length in the dark night?

Pegeen: (*impatiently*) He is surely, and leaving me lonesome on the scruff of the hill. (*She gets up and puts envelope on dresser, then winds clock.*) Isn't it long the nights are now, Shawn Keogh, to be leaving a poor girl with her own self counting the hours to the dawn of day?

Shawn: (*with awkward humour*) If it is, when we're wedded in a short while you'll have no call to complain, for I've little will to be walking off to wakes or weddings in the darkness of the night.

Pegeen: (*with rather scornful good humour*) You're making mighty certain, Shaneen, that I'll wed you now.

Shawn: Aren't we after making a good bargain, the way we're only waiting these days on Father Reilly's dispensation from the bishops, or the Court of Rome.

Pegeen: (*looking at him teasingly, washing up at dresser*) It's a wonder, Shaneen, the Holy Father'd be taking notice of the likes of you; for if I was him I wouldn't bother with this place where you'll meet none but Red Linahan, has a squint in his eye, and Patcheen is lame in his heel, or the mad Mulrannies were driven from California and

	they lost in their wits. We're a queer lot these times to go troubling the Holy Father on his sacred seat.
Shawn:	*(scandalized)* If we are, we're as good this place as another, maybe, and as good these times as we were for ever.
Pegeen:	*(with scorn)* As good, is it? Where now will you meet the like of Daneen Sullivan knocked the eye from a peeler, or Marcus Quin, God rest him, got six months for maiming ewes, and he a great warrant to tell stories of holy Ireland till he'd have the old women shedding down tears about their feet. Where will you find the like of them, I'm saying?
Shawn:	*(timidly)* If you don't it's a good job, maybe; for *(with peculiar emphasis on the words)* Father Reilly has small conceit to have that kind walking around and talking to the girls.
Pegeen:	*(impatiently, throwing water from basin out of the door)* Stop tormenting me with Father Reilly *(imitating his voice)* when I'm asking only what way I'll pass these twelve hours of dark, and not take my death with the fear. *(Looking out of door)*
Shawn:	*(timidly)* Would I fetch you the Widow Quin, maybe?
Pegeen:	Is it the like of that murderer? You'll not, surely.
Shawn:	*(going to her, soothingly)* Then I'm thinking himself will stop along with you when he sees you taking on, for it'll be a long night-time with great darkness, and I'm after feeling a kind of fellow above in the furzy ditch, groaning wicked like a maddening dog, the way it's good cause you have, maybe, to be fearing now.
Pegeen:	*(turning on him sharply)* What's that? Is it a man you seen?
Shawn:	*(retreating)* I couldn't see him at all; but I heard him groaning out, and breaking his heart. It should have been a young man from his words speaking.
Pegeen:	*(going after him)* And you never went near to see was he hurted or what ailed him at all?
Shawn:	I did not, Pegeen Mike. It was a dark, lonesome place to be hearing the like of him.
Pegeen:	Well, you're a daring fellow, and if they find his corpse stretched above in the dews of dawn, what'll you say then to the peelers, or the Justice of the Peace?
Shawn:	*(thunderstruck)* I wasn't thinking of that. For the love of God, Pegeen Mike, don't let on I was speaking of him. Don't tell your father and the men is coming above; for if they heard that story, they'd have great blabbing this night at the wake.
Pegeen:	I'll maybe tell them, and I'll maybe not.
Shawn:	They are coming at the door, Will you whisht, I'm saying?
Pegeen:	Whisht yourself.
	(She goes behind counter. Michael James, fat jovial publican, comes in followed by Philly Cullen, who is thin and mistrusting, and Jimmy Farrell, who is fat and amorous, about forty-five)
Men:	*(together)* God bless you. The blessing of God on this place.
Pegeen:	God bless you kindly.

Michael: (*to men who go to the counter*) Sit down now, and take your rest. (*Crosses to Shawn at the fire.*) And how is it you are, Shawn Keogh? Are you coming over the sands to Kate Cassidy's wake?

Shawn: I am not, Michael James. I'm going home the short cut to my bed.

Pegeen: (*speaking across the counter*) He's right too, and have you no shame, Michael James, to be quitting off for the whole night, and leaving myself lonesome in the shop?

Michael: (*good-humouredly*) Isn't it the same whether I go for the whole night or a part only? And I'm thinking it's a queer daughter you are if you'd have me crossing backward through the Stooks of the Dead Women, with a drop taken.

Pegeen: If I am a queer daughter, it's a queer father'd be leaving me lonesome these twelve hours of dark, and I piling the turf with the dogs barking, and the calves mooing, and my own teeth rattling with the fear.

Jimmy: (*flatteringly*) What is there to hurt you, and you a fine, hardy girl would knock the head of any two men in the place?

Pegeen: (*working herself up*) Isn't there the harvest boys with their tongues red for drink, and the ten tinkers is camped in the east glen, and the thousand militia — bad cuss to them! — walking idle through the land. There's lots surely to hurt me, and I won't stop alone in it, let himself do what he will.

Michael: If you're that afeard, let Shawn Keogh stop along with you. It's the will of God, I'm thinking, himself should be seeing to you now. (*They all turn on Shawn*)

Shawn: (*in horrified confusion*) I would and welcome, Michael James, but I'm afeard of Father Reilly; and what at all would the Holy Father and the Cardinals of Rome be saying if they heard I did the like of that?

Michael: (*with contempt*) God help you! Can't you sit in by the hearth with the light lit and herself beyond in the room? You'll do that surely, for I've heard tell there's a queer fellow above, going mad or getting his death, maybe, in the gripe of the ditch, so she'd be safer this night with a person here.

Shawn: (*with plaintive despair*) I'm afeard of Father Reilly, I'm saying. Let you not be tempting me, and we near married itself.

Philly: (*with cold contempt*) Lock him in the west room. He'll stay then and have no sin to be telling to the priest.

Michael: (*to Shawn, getting between him and the door*) Go up now.

Shawn: (*at the top of his voice*) Don't stop me, Michael James. Let me out of the door, I'm saying, for the love of the Almighty God. Let me out (*trying to dodge past him*). Let me out of it, and may God grant you His indulgence in the hour of need.

Michael: (*loudly*) Stop your noising, and sit down by the hearth. (*Gives him a push and goes to counter laughing*)

Shawn: (*turning back, wringing his hands*) Oh, Father Reilly and the saints of God, where will I hide myself to-day? Oh, St. Joseph and St. Patrick and St. Brigid, and St. James, have mercy on me now! (*Shawn turns round, sees door clear, and makes a rush for it.*)

Michael: (*catching him by the coattail*) You'd be going, is it?

> **Shawn:** (*screaming*) Leave me go, Michael James, leave me go, you old Pagan, leave me go, or I'll get the curse of the priests on you, and of the scarlet-coated bishops of the courts of Rome. (*With a sudden movement he pulls himself out of his coat, and disappears out of the door, leaving his coat in Michael's hands*)
>
> **Michael:** (*turning round, and holding up coat*) Well, there's the coat of a Christian man. Oh, there's sainted glory this day in the lonesome west; and by the will of God I've got you a decent man, Pegeen, you'll have no call to be spying after if you've a score of young girls, maybe, weeding in your fields.
>
> **Pegeen:** (*taking up the defense of her property*) What right have you to be making game of a poor fellow for minding the priest, when it's your own the fault is, not paying a penny pot-boy to stand along with me and give me courage in the doing of my work? (*She snaps the coat away from him, and goes behind counter with it*)

(a) Pegeen is angry with her father. Explain her reasons for this.

_____
_____
_____

(b) What does she want Shawn to do to fix the situation?

_____
_____
_____

(c) What reason does Shawn give for refusing to help and what alternative does he suggest?

_____
_____
_____

(d) Shawn and Pegeen are waiting to get married. What are they waiting for?

_____
_____

(e) Pegeen criticises some of the other people that live in the village. Explain what crimes, according to Pegeen, the following people have committed:

- Daneen Sullivan: _____
_____
_____

- Marcus Quin: _____

- Widow Quin: _____

(f) What do the other men in the pub think of Shawn? Explain your answer.

_____

(g) Pegeen's attitude to Shawn changes dramatically when he leaves the pub. Explain how she behaved towards him (i) before he left and (ii) after he was gone.

(i) _____

(ii) _____

(h) Why do you think her attitude changed?

_____

(i) Use three adjectives to describe Pegeen's character. Explain each of your choices.

- _____

- _____

- ○ _____

(j) Use three adjectives to describe Shawn's character. Explain each of your choices.

- ○ _____

- ○ _____

- ○ _____

(k) Imagine you are putting on a production of this play. Describe the costumes of the following characters and say why you chose them:

- ○ Pegeen: _____

- ○ Michael: _____

- ○ Shawn: _____

(l) If you were putting on a production of this play, describe what the set would look like.

_____

(m) How would you light the stage? Explain your answer.

PRACTICAL EXERCISE!

In woodwork or art class, create a model of a set for *The Playboy of the Western World*. Research on the Internet for ideas or images that might be useful. In English class, read the stage directions carefully and make a list of anything that is required from the set. Look at the sample set below. How could you improve it? 🙂

STANDARD ASSIGNMENT

Conduct a close study of a play. Keep samples of your own creative writing in relation to drama.

3. Look at how the extract of *The Playboy of the Western World* ended. Continue the dialogue that you imagine might have taken place between Pegeen and her father after Shawn left. Write the dialogue below.

Comparing Different Forms of Drama

4. Read the extracts from *Only Fools and Horses* and *The Playboy of the Western World* again. Answer the questions below.

    (a) What would you say are the main differences between television drama and stage performances?

(b) What difficulties can arise in a stage production that could be overcome easily in a televised version?

(c) Compare the dialogue in the two dramas. What is similar about the dialogue? What is different?

(d) Which of the two dramas do you prefer? Explain your answer.

(e) Would you prefer to go and see a live performance of a drama, or watch it on television? Give two fully explained reasons for your answer.

-

-

🛠 PRACTICAL EXERCISE!

Go to the theatre to see a live performance. Remember to pay attention to the costume, setting, lighting and characterisation. Enjoy the show! ☺

On your return, use a computer to write a report on your experience. Did you enjoy the play? Would you go to the theatre again? Why? Why not? ☺

CHAPTER 19 Film Studies

Recommended Films

Here is a list of some of the films you might choose to watch in order to complete this section:

- *My Left Foot* directed by Jim Sheridan.
- *The Usual Suspects* directed by Bryan Singer.
- *The Shawshank Redemption* directed by Frank Darabont.
- *Edward Scissorhands* directed by Tim Burton.
- *Into the West* directed by Mike Newell.
- *Little Miss Sunshine* directed by Jonathan Dayton and Valerie Faris.

1. Select a film to watch in class. Make sure it is suitably age rated for your class group.

Before watching the film

(a) Examine the DVD case. From your reading of the blurb, describe the plot.

_____
_____
_____
_____

(b) To what genre does this film belong?

_____
_____
_____

(c) What does the illustration on the case tell you about the film? Explain your answer.

_____
_____
_____
_____
_____

(d) Who do you think is the target audience for this film? Give reasons for your answer.

_____
_____
_____
_____

(e) Who do you think will be the main character in the film? Why do you think so?

_____
_____
_____
_____

(f) Fill in the following details about the film:

- running time _____
- age rating _____
- director _____

After watching the film

(g) Explain the plot of the film.

_____
_____
_____
_____
_____

(h) What is the main theme?

_____
_____
_____

(i) Describe the main character.

_____
_____
_____
_____

(j) How well did the main actor play his or her character? Explain your answer.

(k) What message do you think the director was trying to convey?

(l) Did the director succeed in doing what he/she set out to achieve? Explain your answer.

(m) You read the DVD case before watching the film. Did the film live up to your expectations or did it disappoint you? Explain your answer.

(n) Name two types of camera shot. From your chosen film, select an example of each type of shot and say whether or not you found it effective.

-
-

STANDARD ASSIGNMENT

Conduct a close study of a film. Keep samples of your own creative writing in relation to film.

2. Write a review of the film you watched in class for publication in your school magazine.

INCORPORATING I.T.

Use a computer to type your review. Why not create a review magazine with one review from everybody in your class? You can use Microsoft Publisher or a similar program to create your magazine. ☺

PRACTICAL EXERCISE!

- Make a short film with your class. Write a script, choose your actors and director and record the performance with a camcorder. You can do as many takes as you need to get it right! Then edit your film using Microsoft Movie Maker or a similar program. You could even include a soundtrack! ☺

- Take a class trip to the cinema. Write a report on the whole experience. ☺

End of Module Checklist: Critical Literacy and Composition

At the end of this module you should have a copy of **each** of the following in your folder to ensure you gain full credits. It is important that you use I.T. wherever possible.

- A short **SONG** you composed that expresses an emotion very important to you.

- An **ARTICLE** for a school magazine, outlining what this particular song means to you.

- A short **POEM** on the theme of hope.

- A **REVIEW** of a short story for your school magazine.

- A **REPORT** on the differences and similarities between a novel and its film version.

CHAPTER 20 Revision

Preparation for the Oral Examination

What is the Oral Examination?

As part of the Leaving Certificate Applied Programme, you will sit an oral test: an interview with an external examiner appointed by the State Examinations Commission. It lasts approximately fifteen minutes and each student is examined individually.

What will the questions be about?

There are four areas for examination. These are:

- Communications and the Working World.
- Communications and Enterprise.
- The Communications Media.
- Critical Literacy and Composition.

What is the examiner looking for?

You will be marked according to the following:

- Your knowledge and understanding of the topics you speak about.
- How much detail you give in responding to the questions.
- Your ability to involve yourself in a genuine two-way communication, both listening and speaking.
- How clear your language is and how well you express yourself.
- Your attitude, stance, eye-contact and general body language.

> **WORKING IN PAIRS, ASK YOUR PARTNER A SELECTION OF THE FOLLOWING QUESTIONS. WHAT ADVICE WOULD YOU GIVE TO HELP HIM OR HER IMPROVE?**

Communication and the Working World

Work experience

- Where did you go on work experience?
- Who organised your work experience?

- Why did you choose this work placement?
- How did you prepare for your work experience?
- What was your first impression of your work place and colleagues?
- What were you expected to do?
- What qualities have you developed through your work experience?
- Describe a typical day at that workplace.

Differences between work and school

- What are the main differences between school and work?
- What are the main differences between being a student and a worker?
- Does school prepare you for working life? Why? Why not?

The skills required for work

- Where would you look for a job?
- When a question on a job application form does not apply to you, what do you write in the space?
- Describe how you would write a formal letter of application.
- What details should you include in your CV?
- What rules did you find difficult to obey while on work experience?
- What should you do if you cannot attend work?
- What kinds of behaviour do you think an employer would regard as appropriate or inappropriate?
- What did you say when you answered the telephone at work?
- What tone of voice did you use?
- How did you get along with other staff members?
- What would you do if a customer has a complaint?
- What advice would you give to other students regarding work experience?

Communication and Enterprise

Mini-company

- What enterprise did your class undertake?
- What product or service did you provide?

- What was the name of your company?
- How did you decide on your product or service?

- What was your role in this company?
- What were your main duties?
- Where did you get the money to set up the company?

- What is market research?
- How did you advertise your enterprise?
- Who was your target market?
- Did you make a profit?

- Why is it important to hold regular meetings in a company?
- Why is it important to keep records of meetings?
- What did you learn from running an enterprise?

The Communications Media

Newspapers

- What are the different types of newspaper?
- What is a broadsheet? What is a tabloid? Give examples.
- What is the difference in news coverage in a broadsheet and a tabloid?
- Do you read the newspaper? Why? Why not?
- How important do you think colour is in a newspaper?
- What is the role of your local newspaper within your community?

Radio

- What is your favourite radio station?
- Why do you think people listen to the radio?
- Identify some of the different types of radio programme.

- Compare a national radio station and a local radio station.
- Why do you think phone-in programmes are so popular?

Television

- What channel do you watch most often? Why?
- Why do you think time slots are so important?
- What programme would you select for teatime viewing? Why?
- Why do you think soap operas are so popular?
- Describe a recent television programme that you watched.

Critical Literacy and Composition

Poetry and lyrics

- What is your favourite song or poem?
- Can you explain its meaning?
- How does the music suit the lyrics?
- Can you remember a particular line from the song or poem? Explain what that line means to you.

Novel and short story

- What is your favourite novel or short story?
- Why do you like it?
- Explain the plot.
- What is the main character like?
- What are the main elements of a good short story or novel?

Drama and film

- Have you attended a live performance of a drama? Did you enjoy it?
- Why do you think lighting and costumes are so important in drama?
- What is meant by: visual qualities, shot sequence and special effects?
- If you were writing a review of a film, what would you highlight?
- What are the main film genres?
- What would you regard as a good film?

- Who is your favourite actor? Why?
- What is the role of a director?
- What does music contribute to a film?
- Why is cinema popular despite the availability of DVDs?

GOOD LUCK! ☺

ACKNOWLEDGEMENTS

Extract from *Father Ted, The Complete Series* by Graham Linehan and Arthur Mathews reprinted by permission of Hat Trick Productions. Article 'Delayed diagnoses could lead to hospital being sued' by Carol Soulter and *Radio listings for RTE Radio 1 and RTE 2 FM* , both from 15.3.2010, reprinted by permission of The Irish Times. Article 'Disgraceful and Unacceptable' by Gary Meneely, The Irish Sun, 15.3.2010, reprinted by permission of NI Syndication. *Television Listings for TV3* reprinted by permission of the Irish Daily Star Chic. Film guide *Top 10 DVDs* reprinted by permission of Heat magazine. Lyrics 'Spanish Train' by Chris de Burgh, Crysalis Music Limited, reprinted by permission of Music Sales Limited. Lyrics 'Luka' by Suzanne Vega reprinted by permission of Warner/Chappell Music Ltd. 'Nothing Gold Can Stay' from the book, *The Poetry of Robert Frost* edited by Edward Connery Lathem. Copyright 1923, 1969 by Henry Holt and Company. Copyright 1951 by Robert Frost. Reprinted by arrangement with Henry Holt and Company, LLC. (digital) 'Nothing Gold Can Stay' from The Poetry of Robert Frost edited by Edward Connery Lathem, published by Jonathan Cape. Reprinted by permission of The Random House Group Ltd. Extract from *My Oedipus Complex and Other Stories* by Frank O'Connor (Penguin Books 1963, 2001). Copyright ©Frank O'Connor, 1963, 2001. Reproduced by permission of Penguin Books Ltd. Extract from Of Mice and Men by John Steinbeck reprinted by permission of Curtis Brown. Extract from *Only Fools and Horses* reprinted by permission of Shazam Productions. Extract from *The Playboy of the Western World* by J.M. Synge reprinted by permission of the Board of Trinity College Dublin.

For permission to reproduce audio content:
Track 1, 'Clair de Lune' by Claude Debussy. Licenced courtesy of Naxos Rights International.
Tracks 6 and 7 are courtesy of RTÉ Libraries and Archives.